CONCISE·
THEOLOGY

A GUIDE TO
HISTORIC
CHRISTIAN
BELIEFS

J. I. PACKER

┼2͟3̶ 52

Tyndale House Publishers, Inc.
WHEATON, ILLINOIS

The "NIV" and "New International Version" trademarks are registered in the United States Patent and Trademark Office by International Bible Society.

The chapters in *Concise Theology* were originally written as extended notes for the New Geneva Study Bible, a project of the Foundation for Reformation, 400 East South Street, Suite 301, Orlando, Florida 32801.

Unless otherwise indicated, all Scripture quotations are taken from the *Holy Bible,* New International Version® NIV®. Copyright © 1973, 1978, 1984 by International Bible Society. Used by permission of Zondervan Publishing House. All rights reserved.

Scripture quotations marked NRSV are from the New Revised Standard Version of the Bible, copyrighted, 1989 by the Division of Christian Education of the National Council of the Churches of Christ in the United States of America, and are used by permission. All rights reserved.

Library of Congress Cataloging-in-Publication Data

Packer, J. I. (James Innell)
  Concise theology : a guide to historic Christian beliefs / J. I. Packer
    p.   cm.
  ISBN 0-8423-1111-4 (HC); 08423-3960-4 (SC)
  1. Theology, Doctrinal—Introductions.   I. Title.

BT65.P33   1993
230'.044—dc20   92-37771

Printed in the United States of America

06   05   04   03   02   01
10   9   8   7   6   5   4   3

Contents

TWO: GOD REVEALED AS REDEEMER

THREE: GOD REVEALED AS LORD OF GRACE

FOUR: GOD REVEALED AS LORD OF DESTINY

Preface

THIS BOOK SETS OUT IN SHORT COMPASS what seem to me to be the permanent essentials of Christianity, viewed as both a belief system and a way of life. Others have other ideas of how Christianity should be profiled, but this is mine. It is Reformational and evangelical, and as such, so I maintain, historic and classic mainstream.

These briefings, which were first planned for a study Bible and have now been revised, have an intentionally scriptural cast and, like other of my writings, are peppered with texts to look up. I submit that this is how it should be, for it is basic to Christianity to receive biblical teaching as God's own instruction, proceeding, as Calvin put it, via human agency from God's holy mouth. If Scripture is indeed God himself preaching and teaching, as the great body of the church has always held, then the first mark of good theology is that it seeks to echo the divine Word as faithfully as it can.

Theology is first the activity of thinking and speaking about God (theologizing), and second the product of that activity (Luther's theology, or Wesley's, or Finney's, or Wimber's, or Packer's, or whoever's). As an activity, theology is a cat's cradle of interrelated though distinct disciplines: elucidating texts (exegesis), synthesizing what they say on the things they deal with (biblical theology), seeing how the faith was stated in the past (historical theology), formulating it for today (systematic theology), finding its implications for conduct (ethics), commending and defending it as truth and wisdom (apologetics), defining the Christian task in the world (missiology), stockpiling resources for life in Christ (spirituality) and corporate worship (liturgy), and exploring ministry (practical theology). The following chapters, sketchy as they are, range into all these areas.

Remembering that the Lord Jesus Christ called those he wanted fed *sheep* rather than *giraffes*, I have aimed to keep things as simple as possible. Archbishop William Temple was once told that he had made a complex issue very simple; he was hugely delighted, and said at once: "Lord, who made me simple, make me simpler yet." My heart goes with Temple's, and I have tried to keep my head in line with it.

As I often tell my students, theology is for doxology and devotion—that is, the praise of God and the practice of godliness. It should therefore be presented in a way that brings awareness of the divine presence. Theology is at its healthiest when it is consciously under the eye of the God of whom it speaks, and when it is singing to his glory. This, too, I have tried to bear in mind.

These short studies of great subjects feel to me, now that I have done them, rather like the lightning tours of England that enterprising bus companies run for American visitors (fifteen minutes at Stonehenge, two hours in Oxford, theatre and overnight in Stratford, an hour and a half in York, an afternoon in the Lake District—*phew!*). Each chapter is a mere sketchy note. Yet I dare to hope that my compressed material, Packer-packed as it is, might expand in readers' minds to lift their hearts Godward, in the way that a different form of hot air lifts balloons and their passengers skyward. We shall see.

My frequent quoting of the Westminster Confession may raise some eyebrows, since I am an Anglican and not a Presbyterian. But since the Confession was intended to amplify the Thirty-nine Articles, and most of its framers were Anglican clergy, and since it is something of a masterpiece, "the ripest fruit of Reformation creed-making" as B. B. Warfield called it, I think I am entitled to value it as part of my Reformed Anglican heritage, and to use it as a major resource.

I gratefully acknowledge the hidden hand of my much-admired friend R. C. Sproul, from whom came the germ idea for several of these outlines. Though our styles differ, we think very much alike, and have cooperated happily in a number of projects. I find that we are sometimes referred to as the Reformed Mafia, but hard words break no bones, and on we go.

Thanks are also due to Wendell Hawley, my publisher, and LaVonne Neff, my editor, for helpfulness and patience in many forms. To work with them has been a privilege and a pleasure.

J. I. PACKER

PART ONE:
GOD REVEALED AS CREATOR

REVELATION

SCRIPTURE IS THE WORD OF GOD

The tablets were the work of God;
the writing was the writing of God,
engraved on the tablets.

EXODUS 32:16

✝ Christianity is the true worship and service of the true God, humankind's Creator and Redeemer. It is a religion that rests on revelation: nobody would know the truth about God, or be able to relate to him in a personal way, had not God first acted to make himself known. But God has so acted, and the sixty-six books of the Bible, thirty-nine written before Christ came and twenty-seven after, are together the record, interpretation, expression, and embodiment of his self-disclosure. God and godliness are the Bible's uniting themes.

From one standpoint, the Scriptures (*Scriptures* means "writings") are the faithful testimony of the godly to the God whom they loved and served; from another standpoint, through a unique exercise of divine overruling in their composition, they are God's own testimony and teaching in human form. The church calls these writings the Word of God because their authorship and contents are both divine.

Decisive assurance that Scripture is from God and consists entirely of his wisdom and truth comes from Jesus

3

Christ and his apostles, who taught in his name. Jesus, God incarnate, viewed his Bible (our Old Testament) as his heavenly Father's written instruction, which he no less than others must obey (Matt. 4:4, 7, 10; 5:19-20; 19:4-6; 26:31, 52-54; Luke 4:16-21; 16:17; 18:31-33; 22:37; 24:25-27, 45-47; John 10:35), and which he had come to fulfill (Matt. 5:17-18; 26:24; John 5:46). Paul described the Old Testament as entirely "God-breathed"—that is, a product of God's Spirit ("breath") just as the cosmos is (Ps. 33:6; Gen. 1:2)—and written to teach Christianity (2 Tim. 3:15-17; Rom. 15:4; 1 Cor. 10:11). Peter affirms the divine origin of biblical teaching in 2 Peter 1:21 and 1 Peter 1:10-12, and so also by his manner of quoting does the writer to the Hebrews (Heb. 1:5-13; 3:7; 4:3; 10:5-7, 15-17; cf. Acts 4:25; 28:25-27).

Since the apostles' teaching about Christ is itself revealed truth in God-taught words (1 Cor. 2:12-13), the church rightly regards authentic apostolic writings as completing the Scriptures. Already Peter refers to Paul's letters as Scripture (2 Pet. 3:15-16), and Paul is apparently calling Luke's gospel Scripture in 1 Timothy 5:18, where he quotes the words of Luke 10:7.

The idea of written directives from God himself as a basis for godly living goes back to God's act of inscribing the Decalogue on stone tablets and then prompting Moses to write his laws and the history of his dealings with his people (Exod. 32:15-16; 34:1, 27-28; Num. 33:2; Deut. 31:9). Digesting and living by this material was always central to true devotion in Israel for both leaders and ordinary people (Josh. 1:7-8; 2 Kings 17:13; 22:8-13; 1 Chron. 22:12-13; Neh. 8; Ps. 119). The principle that all must be governed by the Scriptures, that is, by the Old and New Testaments taken together, is equally basic to Christianity.

What Scripture says, God says; for, in a manner comparable only to the deeper mystery of the Incarnation, the Bible is both fully human and fully divine. So all its manifold contents—histories, prophecies, poems, songs, wisdom writings, sermons, statistics, letters, and whatever else—should be received as from God, and all that Bible writers teach should be revered as God's authoritative instruction. Christians should be grateful to God for the gift of his written Word, and conscientious in basing their faith and life entirely and exclusively upon it. Otherwise, we cannot ever honor or please him as he calls us to do.

INTERPRETATION
CHRISTIANS CAN UNDERSTAND THE WORD OF GOD

*Give me understanding, and I will keep
your law and obey it with all my heart.*

PSALM 119:34

✝ All Christians have a right and duty not only to learn from the church's heritage of faith but also to interpret Scripture for themselves. The church of Rome doubts this, alleging that individuals easily misinterpret the Scriptures. This is true; but the following rules, faithfully observed, will help prevent that from happening.

Every book of Scripture is a human composition, and though it should always be revered as the Word of God, interpretation of it must start from its human character. Allegorizing, therefore, which disregards the human writer's expressed meaning is never appropriate.

Each book was written not in code but in a way that could be understood by the readership to which it was addressed. This is true even of the books that primarily use symbolism: Daniel, Zechariah, and Revelation. The main thrust is always clear, even if details are clouded. So when we understand the words used, the historical background, and the cultural conventions of the writer and his readers, we are well on the way to grasping the thoughts that are being conveyed. Spiritual understanding—that is, the dis-

6

cernment of the reality of God, his ways with humankind, his present will, and one's own relationship to him now and for the future—will not however reach us from the text until the veil is removed from our hearts and we are able to share the writer's own passion to know and please and honor God (2 Cor. 3:16; 1 Cor. 2:14). Prayer that God's Spirit may generate this passion in us and show us God in the text is needed here. (See Ps. 119:18-19, 26-27, 33-34, 73, 125, 144, 169; Eph. 1:17-19; 3:16-19.)

Each book had its place in the progress of God's revelation of grace, which began in Eden and reached its climax in Jesus Christ, Pentecost, and the apostolic New Testament. That place must be borne in mind when studying the text. The Psalms, for instance, model the godly heart in every age, but express its prayers and praises in terms of the typical realities (earthly kings, kingdoms, health, wealth, war, long life) that circumscribed the life of grace in the pre-Christian era.

Each book proceeded from the same divine mind, so the teaching of the Bible's sixty-six books will be complementary and self-consistent. If we cannot yet see this, the fault is in us, not in Scripture. It is certain that Scripture nowhere contradicts Scripture; rather, one passage explains another. This sound principle of interpreting Scripture by Scripture is sometimes called the analogy of Scripture or the analogy of faith.

Each book exhibits unchanging truth about God, humanity, godliness, and ungodliness, applied to and illustrated by particular situations in which individuals and groups found themselves. The final stage in biblical interpretation is to reapply these truths to our own life-situations; this is the way to discern what God in Scripture is saying to us at this moment. Examples of such reapplication are Josiah's realization of God's wrath at Judah's failure to observe his law (2 Kings 22:8-13), Jesus' reasoning from Genesis 2:24 (Matt. 19:4-6), and Paul's use of Genesis 15:6 and Psalm 32:1-2 to show the reality of present righteousness by faith (Rom. 4:1-8).

No meaning may be read into or imposed on Scripture that cannot with certainty be read out of Scripture—shown, that is, to be unambiguously expressed by one or more of the human writers.

Careful and prayerful observance of these rules is a mark of every Christian who "correctly handles the word of truth" (2 Tim. 2:15).

GENERAL
REVELATION

GOD'S REALITY IS KNOWN TO ALL

The heavens declare the glory of God;
the skies proclaim the work of his hands.

PSALM 19:1

✠ God's world is not a shield hiding the Creator's power and majesty. From the natural order it is evident that a mighty and majestic Creator is there. Paul says this in Romans 1:19-21, and in Acts 17:28 he calls a Greek poet as witness that humans are divinely created. Paul also affirms that the goodness of this Creator becomes evident from kindly providences (Acts 14:17; cf. Rom. 2:4), and that some at least of the demands of his holy law are known to every human conscience (Rom. 2:14-15), along with the uncomfortable certainty of eventual retributive judgment (Rom. 1:32). These evident certainties constitute the content of general revelation.

General revelation is so called because everyone receives it, just by virtue of being alive in God's world. This has been so from the start of human history. God actively discloses these aspects of himself to all human beings, so that in every case failure to thank and serve the Creator in righteousness is sin against knowledge, and denials of having received this knowledge should not be taken seriously. God's universal revelation of his power, praiseworthiness, and moral claim is the basis of Paul's indictment of the whole human race as sinful and guilty before God for failing to serve him as we should (Rom. 1:18–3:19).

God has now supplemented general revelation with the further revelation of himself as Savior of sinners through Jesus Christ. This revelation, given in history and embodied in Scripture, and opening the door of salvation to the lost, is usually called special or specific revelation. It includes explicit verbal statement of all that general revelation tells us about God, and teaches us to recognize that revelation in the natural order, in the events of history, and in the makeup of human beings, so that we learn to see the entire world as, in Calvin's phrase, a theatre of the glory of God.

GUILT

THE EFFECT OF GENERAL REVELATION

*. . . what may be known about God
is plain to them, because God has made it
plain to them.*

ROMANS 1:19

✚ Scripture assumes, and experience confirms, that human beings are naturally inclined to some form of religion, yet they fail to worship their Creator, whose general revelation of himself makes him universally known. Both theoretical atheism and moral monotheism are natural to no one: atheism is always a reaction against a pre-existing belief in God or gods, and moral monotheism has only ever appeared in the wake of special revelation.

Scripture explains this state of affairs by telling us that sinful egoism and aversion to our Creator's claims drive humankind into idolatry, which means transferring worship and homage to some power or object other than God the Creator (Isa. 44:9-20; Rom. 1:21-23; Col. 3:5). In this way, apostate humans "suppress the truth" and have "exchanged the glory of the immortal God for images made to look like mortal man and birds and animals and reptiles" (Rom. 1:18, 23). They smother and quench, as far as they can, the awareness that general revelation gives them

11

of the transcendent Creator-Judge, and attach their in-eradicable sense of deity to unworthy objects. This in turn leads to drastic moral decline, with consequent misery, as a first manifestation of God's wrath against human apostasy (Rom. 1:18, 24-32).

Nowadays in the West people idolize and, in effect, worship secular objects such as the firm, the family, football, and pleasant feelings of various kinds. But moral decline still results, just as it did when pagans worshipped literal idols in Bible times.

Human beings cannot entirely suppress their sense of God and his present and future judgment; God himself will not let them do that. Some sense of right and wrong, as well as of being accountable to a holy divine Judge, always remains. In our fallen world all whose minds are not in some way impaired have a conscience that at some points directs them and from time to time condemns them, telling them that they ought to suffer for wrongs they have done (Rom. 2:14ff.); and when conscience speaks in these terms it is in truth the voice of God.

Fallen humankind is in one sense ignorant of God, since what people like to believe, and do in fact believe, about the objects of their worship falsifies and distorts the revelation of God they cannot escape. In another sense, however, all human beings remain aware of God, guiltily, with uncomfortable inklings of coming judgment that they wish they did not have. Only the gospel of Christ can speak peace to this distressful aspect of the human condition.

INWARD WITNESS

SCRIPTURE IS AUTHENTICATED BY THE HOLY SPIRIT

But you have an anointing from the Holy One,
and all of you know the truth.

1 JOHN 2:20

✝ Why do Christians believe that the Bible is the Word of God, sixty-six books forming a single book of instruction in which God reveals to us the reality of redemption through Jesus Christ the Savior? The answer is that God himself has confirmed this through what is called the inward witness of the Holy Spirit. In the words of the Westminster Confession (1647):

We may be moved and induced by the testimony of the Church to an high and reverend esteem of the Holy Scripture. And the heavenliness of the matter, the efficacy of the doctrine, the majesty of the style, the consent of all the parts, the scope of the whole (which is, to give all glory to God), the full discovery it makes of the only way of man's salvation, the many other incomparable excellencies, and the entire perfection thereof, are arguments whereby it doth abundantly evidence itself to be the Word of God: yet notwithstanding, our full persuasion and assurance of the infallible truth and divine authority thereof, is from the inward work of the Holy Spirit bearing witness by and with the Word in our heart. (I.5)

The Spirit's witness to Scripture is like his witness to Jesus, which we find spoken of in John 15:26 and 1 John

5:7 (cf. 1 John 2:20, 27). It is a matter not of imparting new information but of enlightening previously darkened minds to discern divinity through sensing its unique impact—the impact in the one case of the Jesus of the gospel, and in the other case of the words of Holy Scripture. The Spirit shines in our hearts to give us the light of the knowledge of the glory of God not only in the face of Jesus Christ (2 Cor. 4:6) but also in the teaching of Holy Scripture. The result of this witness is a state of mind in which both the Savior and the Scriptures have evidenced themselves to us as divine—Jesus, a divine person; Scripture, a divine product—in a way as direct, immediate, and arresting as that in which tastes and colors evidence themselves by forcing themselves on our senses. In consequence, we no longer find it possible to doubt the divinity of either Christ or the Bible.

Thus God authenticates Holy Scripture to us as his Word—not by some mystical experience or secret information privately whispered into some inner ear, not by human argument alone (strong as this may be), nor by the church's testimony alone (impressive as this is when one looks back over two thousand years). God does it, rather, by means of the searching light and transforming power whereby Scripture evidences itself to be divine. The impact of this light and power is itself the Spirit's witness "by and with the Word in our heart." Argument, testimony from others, and our own particular experiences may prepare us to receive this witness, but the imparting of it, like the imparting of faith in Christ's divine Saviorhood, is the prerogative of the sovereign Holy Spirit alone.

The illumination of the Spirit witnessing to the divinity

of the Bible is universal Christian experience, and has been so from the beginning, though many Christians have not known how to verbalize it or to handle the Bible in a manner consistent with it.

AUTHORITY

GOD GOVERNS HIS PEOPLE
THROUGH SCRIPTURE

All Scripture is God-breathed and is useful
for teaching, rebuking, correcting and
training in righteousness.

2 TIMOTHY 3:16

✝ The Christian principle of biblical authority means, on the one hand, that God purposes to direct the belief and behavior of his people through the revealed truth set forth in Holy Scripture; on the other hand it means that all our ideas about God should be measured, tested, and where necessary corrected and enlarged, by reference to biblical teaching. Authority as such is the right, claim, fitness, and by extension power, to control. Authority in Christianity belongs to God the Creator, who made us to know, love, and serve him, and his way of exercising his authority over us is by means of the truth and wisdom of his written Word. As from the human standpoint each biblical book was written to induce more consistent and wholehearted service of God, so from the divine standpoint the entire Bible has this purpose. And since the Father has now given the Son executive authority to rule the cosmos on his behalf (Matt. 28:18), Scripture now functions precisely as the instrument of Christ's lordship over his followers. All

Scripture is like Christ's letters to the seven churches (Rev. 2–3) in this regard.

Where is God's authoritative truth to be found today? Three answers are given, and each appeals to the Bible in its own way.

The Roman Catholic and Orthodox churches find God's truth, as they believe, in the interpretations of Scripture that are embodied in their own tradition and consensus. They view the Bible as God-given truth, but they insist that the church must interpret it and is infallible when it does so.

By contrast, individuals labeled liberal, radical, modernist, or subjectivist find God's truth in the thoughts, impressions, judgments, theories and speculations that Scripture triggers in their own minds. While dismissing the New Testament concept of the inspiration of Scripture, and not treating their Bible as totally trustworthy or as embodying absolute and authoritative transcripts of the mind of God, they are confident that the Spirit leads them to pick and choose in such a way that wisdom from God results.

Historic Protestantism, however, finds God's truth in the teaching of the canonical Scriptures as such. It receives these Scriptures as inspired (i.e., God-breathed, 2 Tim. 3:16), inerrant (i.e., totally true in all they affirm), sufficient (i.e., telling us all that God wills to tell us and all that we need to know for salvation and eternal life), and clear (i.e., straightforward and self-interpreting on all matters of importance).

The first two positions treat human judgments on the Bible as decisive for truth and wisdom; the third, while valuing the church's heritage of conviction and appreciating the demand for coherence that rational thinking involves, systematically submits all human thoughts to Scripture, which it takes seriously as canon. *Canon* means a rule or standard. The first two positions refer to Scripture as the canon, but they fail to take it with full seriousness as a functioning rule for faith and life. Thus they do not in practice fully accept its authority, and their Christian profession, however sincere, is thereby flawed.

KNOWLEDGE

TRUE KNOWLEDGE OF GOD COMES THROUGH FAITH

"But let him who boasts boast about this: that he understands and knows me, that I am the LORD, who exercises kindness, justice and righteousness on earth, for in these I delight," declares the LORD.

JEREMIAH 9:24

✝ In 1 Timothy 6:20-21 Paul warns Timothy against "what is falsely called knowledge (Greek *gnosis*), which some have professed and in so doing have wandered from the faith." Paul is attacking theosophical and religious tendencies that developed into Gnosticism in the second century A.D. Teachers of these beliefs and practices told believers to see their Christian commitment as a somewhat confused first step along the road to "knowledge," and urged them to take more steps along that road. But these teachers viewed the material order as worthless and the body as a prison for the soul, and they treated illumination as the complete answer to human spiritual need. They denied that sin was any part of the problem, and the "knowledge" they offered had to do only with spells, celestial passwords, and disciplines of mysticism and detachment. They reclassified Jesus as a supernatural teacher who had looked human, though he was not; the

Incarnation and the Atonement they denied, and replaced Christ's call to a life of holy love with either prescriptions for asceticism or permission for licentiousness. Paul's letters to Timothy (1 Tim. 1:3-4; 4:1-7; 6:20-21; 2 Tim. 3:1-9); Jude 4, 8-19; 2 Peter 2; and John's first two letters (1 John 1:5-10; 2:9-11, 18-29; 3:7-10; 4:1-6, 5:1-12; 2 John 7-11) are explicitly opposing beliefs and practices that would later emerge as Gnosticism.

By contrast, Scripture speaks of "knowing" God as the spiritual person's ideal: namely, the fullness of a faith-relationship that brings salvation and eternal life and generates love, hope, obedience, and joy. (See, for example, Exod. 33:13; Jer. 31:34; Heb. 8:8-12; Dan. 11:32; John 17:3; Gal. 4:8-9; Eph. 1:17-19; 3:19; Phil. 3:8-11; 2 Tim. 1:12.) The dimensions of this knowledge are intellectual (knowing the truth about God: Deut. 7:9; Ps. 100:3); volitional (trusting, obeying, and worshiping God in terms of that truth); and moral (practicing justice and love: Jer. 22:16; 1 John 4:7-8). Faith-knowledge focuses on God incarnate, the man Christ Jesus, the mediator between God and us sinners, through whom we come to know his Father as our Father (John 14:6). Faith seeks to know Christ and his power specifically (Phil. 3:8-14). Faith's knowledge is the fruit of regeneration, the bestowal of a new heart (Jer. 24:7; 1 John 5:20), and of illumination by the Spirit (2 Cor. 4:6; Eph. 1:17). The knowledge-relationship is reciprocal, implying covenantal affection on both sides: we know God as ours because he knows us as his (John 10:14; Gal. 4:9; 2 Tim. 2:19).

All Scripture has been given to help us know God in this way. Let us labor to use it for its proper purpose.

CREATION

GOD IS THE CREATOR

How many are your works,
O LORD! In wisdom you made them all;
the earth is full of your creatures.

PSALM 104:24

✝ "In the beginning God created the heavens and the earth" (Gen. 1:1). He did it by fiat, without any preexisting material; his resolve that things should exist ("Let there be . . .") called them into being and formed them in order with an existence that depended on his will yet was distinct from his own. Father, Son, and Holy Spirit were involved together (Gen. 1:2; Pss. 33:6, 9; 148:5; John 1:1-3; Col. 1:15-16; Heb. 1:2; 11:3). Points to note are as follows:

(a) The act of creation is mystery to us; there is more in it than we can understand. We cannot create by fiat, and we do not know how God could. To say that he created "out of nothing" is to confess the mystery, not explain it. In particular, we cannot conceive how dependent existence can be distinct existence, nor how angels and human beings in their dependent existence can be not robots but creatures capable of free decisions for which they are morally accountable to their Maker. Yet Scripture everywhere teaches us that this is the way it is.

(b) Space and time are dimensions of the created order; God is not "in" either; nor is he bound by either as we are.

21

(c) As the world order is not self-created, so it is not self-sustaining, as God is. The stability of the universe depends on constant divine upholding; this is a specific ministry of the divine Son (Col. 1:17; Heb. 1:3), and without it every creature of every kind, ourselves included, would cease to be. As Paul told the Athenians, "he himself gives all men life and breath and everything else. . . . In him we live and move and have our being" (Acts 17:25, 28).

(d) The possibility of creative intrusions (e.g., miracles of creative power; creating new persons through human procreative activity; reorienting human hearts and redirecting human desires and energies in regeneration) is as old as the cosmos itself. How far God in his upholding activity actually continues to create new things that cannot be explained in terms of anything that went before, it is beyond our power to know; but certainly his world remains open to his creative power at every point.

Knowing that God created the world around us, and ourselves as part of it, is basic to true religion. God is to be praised as Creator, by reason of the marvelous order, variety, and beauty of his works. Psalms such as Psalm 104 model this praise. God is to be trusted as the sovereign LORD, with an eternal plan covering all events and destinies without exception, and with power to redeem, re-create and renew; such trust becomes rational when we remember that it is the almighty Creator that we are trusting. Realizing our moment-by-moment dependence on God the Creator for our very existence makes it appropriate to live lives of devotion, commitment, gratitude, and loyalty toward him, and scandalous not to. Godliness starts here, with God the sovereign Creator as the first focus of our thoughts.

SELF-DISCLOSURE

"THIS IS MY NAME"

*God also said to Moses, "Say to the Israelites,
'The LORD, the God of your fathers—the
God of Abraham, the God of Isaac and the
God of Jacob—has sent me to you.' This is
my name forever, the name by which I am to
be remembered from generation to
generation."*

EXODUS 3:15

✝ In the modern world, a person's name is merely an identifying label, like a number, which could be changed without loss. Bible names, however, have their background in the widespread tradition that personal names give information, describing in some way who people are. The Old Testament constantly celebrates the fact that God has made his name known to Israel, and the psalms direct praise to God's name over and over (Pss. 8:1; 113:1-3, 145:1-2, 148:5, 13). "Name" here means God himself as he has revealed himself by word and deed. At the heart of this self-revelation is the name by which he authorized Israel to invoke him—*Yahweh* as modern scholars write it, *Jehovah* as it used to be rendered, *the LORD* as it is printed in English versions of the Old Testament.

God declared this name to Moses when he spoke to him out of the thornbush that burned steadily without being burned up. God began by identifying himself as the God who had committed himself in covenant to the patriarchs (cf. Gen. 17:1-14); then, when Moses asked him what he might tell the people that this God's name was (for the ancient assumption was that prayer would be heard only if you named its addressee correctly), God first said "I AM WHO I AM" (or, "I will be what I will be"), then shortened it to "I AM," and finally called himself "the LORD (Hebrew *Yahweh*, a name sounding like "I AM" in Hebrew), the God of your fathers" (Exod. 3:6, 13-16). The name in all its forms proclaims his eternal, self-sustaining, self-deter-mining, sovereign reality—that supernatural mode of ex-istence that the sign of the burning bush had signified. The bush, we might say, was God's three-dimensional illustration of his own inexhaustible life. "This is my name forever," he said—that is, God's people should always think of him as the living, reigning, potent, unfettered and undiminished king that the burning bush showed him to be (Exod. 3:15).

Later (Exod. 33:18–34:7) Moses asks to see God's "glory" (adorable self-display), and in reply God did "pro-claim his name" thus: "The LORD, the LORD, the com-passionate and gracious God, slow to anger, abounding in love and faithfulness, maintaining love to thousands, and forgiving wickedness, rebellion and sin. Yet he does not leave the guilty unpunished . . ." At the burning bush God had answered the question, In what way does God exist? Here he answers the question, In what way does God behave? This foundational announcement of his moral character is often echoed in later Scriptures (Neh. 9:17; Ps. 86:15; Joel 2:13; John 4:2). It is all part of his "name," that is, his disclosure of his nature, for which he is to be adored forever.

God rounds off this revelation of the glory of his moral character by calling himself "the LORD, whose name is Jealous" (Exod. 34:14). This echoes, with emphasis, what he said of himself in the sanction of the second commandment (Exod. 20:5). The jealousy affirmed is covenantal: it is the virtue of the commited lover, who wants the total loyalty of the one he has bound himself to honor and serve.

In the New Testament, the words and acts of Jesus, the incarnate Son, constitute a full revelation of the mind, outlook, ways, plans, and purposes of God the Father (John 14:9-11; cf. 1:18). "Hallowed be your name" in the Lord's prayer (Matt. 6:9) expresses the desire that the first person of the Godhead will be revered and praised as the splendor of his self-disclosure deserves. God is to be given glory for all the glories of his name, that is, his glorious self-revelation in creation, providence, and grace.

SELF-EXISTENCE

GOD HAS ALWAYS BEEN

*Before the mountains were born or you
brought forth the earth and the world, from
everlasting to everlasting you are God.*

PSALM 90:2

✝ Children sometimes ask, "Who made God?" The clearest answer is that God never needed to be made, because he was always there. He exists in a different way from us: we, his creatures, exist in a dependent, derived, finite, fragile way, but our Maker exists in an eternal, self-sustaining, necessary way—necessary, that is, in the sense that God does not have it in him to go out of existence, just as we do not have it in us to live forever. We necessarily age and die, because it is our present nature to do that; God necessarily continues forever unchanged, because it is his eternal nature to do that. This is one of many contrasts between creature and Creator.

God's self-existence is a basic truth. At the outset of his presentation of the unknown God to the Athenian idolaters, Paul explained that this God, the world's Creator, "is not served by human hands, as if he needed anything, because he himself gives all men life and breath and everything else" (Acts 17:23-25). Sacrifices offered to idols, in today's tribal religions as in ancient Athens, are thought of as somehow keeping the god going, but the Creator needs no such support system. The word *aseity*, meaning that he has life in himself and draws his unending energy from himself (*a se* in Latin means "from himself"), was coined by theologians to express this truth, which the Bible makes clear (Pss. 90:1-4; 102:25-27; Isa. 40:28-31; John 5:26; Rev. 4:10).

In theology, endless mistakes result from supposing that the conditions, bounds, and limits of our own finite existence apply to God. The doctrine of his aseity stands as a bulwark against such mistakes. In our life of faith, we easily impoverish ourselves by embracing an idea of God that is too limited and small, and again the doctrine of God's aseity stands as a bulwark to stop this happening. It is vital for spiritual health to believe that God is great (cf. Ps. 95:1-7), and grasping the truth of his aseity is the first step on the road to doing this.

TRANSCENDENCE
GOD'S NATURE IS SPIRITUAL

This is what the LORD says: "Heaven is my throne, and the earth is my footstool. Where is the house you will build for me? Where will my resting place be?"

ISAIAH 66:1

✝ "God is spirit," said Jesus to the Samaritan woman at the well (John 4:24). Though fully personal, God does not live in and through a body as we do, and so is not anchored in a spatio-temporal frame. From this fact, plus the further fact that he is self-existent and not marked as we are by the personal disintegration (lack of concentration and control) that sin has produced in us, several things follow.

First, God is limited neither by space (he is everywhere in his fullness continually) nor by time (there is no "present moment" into which he is locked as we are). Theologians refer to God's freedom from limits and bounds as his infinity, his immensity, and his transcendence (1 Kings 8:27; Isa. 40:12-26; 66:1). As he upholds everything in being, so he has everything everywhere always before his mind, in its own relation to his all-inclusive plan and purpose for every item and every person in his world (Dan. 4:34-35; Eph. 1:11).

Second, God is immutable. This means that he is totally

consistent: because he is necessarily perfect, he cannot change either for the better or for the worse; and because he is not in time he is not subject to change as creatures are (2 Pet. 3:8). Far from being detached and immobile, he is always active in his world, constantly making new things spring forth (Isa. 42:9; 2 Cor. 5:17; Rev. 21:5); but in all this he expresses his perfect character with perfect consistency. It is precisely the immutability of his character that guarantees his adherence to the words he has spoken and the plans he has made (Num. 23:19; Ps. 33:11; Mal. 3:6; James 1:16-18); and it is this immutability that explains why, when people change their attitude to him, he changes his attitude to them (Gen. 6:5-7; Exod. 32:9-14; 1 Sam. 15:11; Jon. 3:10). The idea that the changelessness of God involves unresponsive indifference to what goes on in his world is the precise opposite of the truth.

Third, God's feelings are not beyond his control, as ours often are. Theologians express this by saying that God is impassible. They mean not that he is impassive and unfeeling but that what he feels, like what he does, is a matter of his own deliberate, voluntary choice and is included in the unity of his infinite being. God is never our victim in the sense that we make him suffer where he had not first chosen to suffer. Scriptures expressing the reality of God's emotions (joy, sorrow, anger, delight, love, hate, etc.) abound, however, and it is a great mistake to forget that God feels—though in a way of necessity that transcends a finite being's experience of emotion.

Fourth, all God's thoughts and actions involve the whole of him. This is his integration, sometimes called his simplicity. It stands in stark contrast to the complexity and lack of integration of our own personal existence, in which, as a result of sin, we are scarcely ever, perhaps never, able to concentrate the whole of our being and all our powers on anything. One aspect of the marvel of God, however, is that he simultaneously gives total and undivided attention not just to one thing at a time but to everything and everyone everywhere in his world past, present, and future (cf. Matt. 10:29-30).

Fifth, the God who is spirit must be worshiped in spirit and in truth, as Jesus said (John 4:24). "In spirit" means "from a heart renewed by the Holy Spirit." No rituals, body movements, or devotional formalities constitute worship without involvement of the heart, which the Holy Spirit alone can induce. "In truth" means "on the basis of God's revelation of reality, which culminates in the incarnate Word, Jesus Christ." First and foremost, this is the revelation of what we are as lost sinners and of what God is to us as Creator-Redeemer through Jesus' mediatorial ministry.

No one place on earth is now prescribed as the only center for worship. God's symbolic dwelling in earthly Jerusalem was replaced when the time came (John 4:23) by his dwelling in heavenly Jerusalem, whence Jesus now ministers (Heb. 12:22-24). In the Spirit, "the LORD is near to all who call on him, to all who call on him in truth," wherever they may be (Ps. 145:18; cf. Heb. 4:14-16). This worldwide availability of God is part of the good news of the gospel; it is a precious benefit, and should not simply be taken for granted.

OMNISCIENCE
GOD SEES AND KNOWS

The eyes of the LORD are everywhere,
keeping watch on the wicked and the good.

PROVERBS 15:3

✝ *Omniscient* is a word that means "knowing everything." Scripture declares that God's eyes run everywhere (Job 24:23; Pss. 33:13-15, 139:13-16; Prov. 15:3;
Jer. 16:17; Heb. 4:13). He searches all hearts and observes
everyone's ways (1 Sam. 16:7; 1 Kings 8:39; 1 Chron. 28:9;
Ps. 139:1-6, 23; Jer. 17:10; Luke 16:15; Rom. 8:27; Rev.
2:23)—in other words, he knows everything about everything and everybody all the time. Also, he knows the
future no less than the past and the present, and possible
events that never happen no less than the actual events that
do (1 Sam. 23:9-13; 2 Kings 13:19; Ps. 81:14-15; Isa.
48:18). Nor does he have to "access" information about
things, as a computer might retrieve a file; all his knowledge is always immediately and directly before his mind.
Bible writers stand in awe of the capacity of God's mind in
this regard (Pss. 139:1-6; 147:5; Isa. 40:13-14, 28; cf. Rom.
11:33-36).

God's knowledge is linked with his sovereignty: he
knows each thing, both in itself and in relation to all other
things, because he created it, sustains it, and now makes it

function every moment according to his plan for it (Eph. 1:11). The idea that God could know, and foreknow, everything without controlling everything seems not only unscriptural but nonsensical.

To the Christian believer, knowledge of God's omniscience brings the assurance that he has not been forgotten, but is being and will be cared for according to God's promise (Isa. 40:27-31). To anyone who is not a Christian, however, the truth of God's universal knowledge must bring dread, for it comes as a reminder that one cannot hide either oneself or one's sins from God's view (Pss. 139:7-12; 94:1-11; John 1:1-12).

SOVEREIGNTY
GOD REIGNS

At the end of that time, I, Nebuchadnezzar,
raised my eyes toward heaven, and my sanity
was restored. Then I praised the Most High;
I honored and glorified him who lives
forever. His dominion is an eternal
dominion; his kingdom endures from
generation to generation.

DANIEL 4:34

✝ The assertion of God's absolute sovereignty in creation, providence, and grace is basic to biblical belief and biblical praise. The vision of God on the throne—that is, ruling—recurs (1 Kings 22:19; Isa. 6:1; Ezek. 1:26; Dan. 7:9; Rev. 4:2; cf. Pss. 11:4; 45:6; 47:8-9; Heb. 12:2; Rev. 3:21); and we are constantly told in explicit terms that the LORD (Yahweh) reigns as king, exercising dominion over great and tiny things alike (Exod. 15:18; Pss. 47; 93; 96:10; 97; 99:1-5; 146:10; Prov. 16:33; 21:1; Isa. 24:23; 52:7; Dan. 4:34-35; 5:21-28; 6:26; Matt. 10:29-31). God's dominion is total: he wills as he chooses and carries out all that he wills, and none can stay his hand or thwart his plans.

That God's rational creatures, angelic and human, have free agency (power of personal decision as to what they shall do) is clear in Scripture throughout; we would not be moral beings, answerable to God the judge, were it not so, nor would it then be possible to distinguish, as Scripture does, between the bad purposes of human agents and the good purposes of God, who sovereignly overrules human action as a planned means to his own goals (Gen. 50:20; Acts 2:23; 13:26-39). Yet the fact of free agency confronts us with mystery, inasmuch as God's control over our free, self-determined activities is as complete as it is over anything else, and how this can be we do not know. Regularly, however, God exercises his sovereignty by letting things take their course, rather than by miraculous intrusions of a disruptive sort.

In Psalm 93 the fact of God's sovereign rule is said to

(a) guarantee the stability of the world against all the forces of chaos (v. 1b-4),
(b) confirm the trustworthiness of all God's utterances and directives (v. 5a), and
(c) call for the homage of holiness on the part of his people (v. 5b). The whole psalm expresses joy, hope, and confidence in God, and no wonder. We shall do well to take its teaching to heart.

ALMIGHTINESS

GOD IS OMNIPRESENT
AND OMNIPOTENT

"Can anyone hide in secret places so that I
cannot see him?" declares the LORD.
"Do not I fill heaven and earth?"
declares the LORD.

JEREMIAH 23:24

✝ God is present in all places; we should not think of
him, however, as filling spaces, for he has no physical dimensions. It is as pure spirit that he pervades all
things, in a relationship of immanence that is more than
we body-bound creatures can understand. One thing that
is clear, however, is that he is present everywhere in the
fullness of all that he is and all the powers that he has, and
needy souls praying to him anywhere in the world receive
the same fullness of his undivided attention. Because God
is omnipresent he is able to give his entire attention to
millions of individuals at the same time. Belief in God's
omnipresence, thus understood, is reflected in Psalm
139:7-10; Jeremiah 23:23-24; Acts 17:24-28. When Paul
speaks of the ascended Christ as filling all things (Eph.
4:8), Christ's availability everywhere in the fullness of his
power is certainly part of the meaning that is being expressed. It is true to say that Father, Son, and Holy Spirit
are today omnipresent together, though the personal pres-

ence of the glorified Son is spiritual (through the Holy Spirit), not physical (in the body).

"I know that you can do all things; no plan of yours can be thwarted" (Job 42:2). Thus Job testifies to the almightiness (omnipotence) of God. Omnipotence means in practice the power to do everything that in his rational and moral perfection (i.e., his wisdom and goodness) God wills to do. This does not mean that God can do literally everything: he cannot sin, lie, change his nature, or deny the demands of his holy character (Num. 23:19; 1 Sam. 15:29; 2 Tim. 2:13; Heb. 6:18; James 1:13, 17); nor can he make a square circle, for the notion of a square circle is self-contradictory; nor can he cease to be God. But all that he wills and promises he can and will do.

Was it excessive for David to say, "I love you, O LORD, my strength. The LORD is my rock, my fortress and my deliverer; my God is my rock, in whom I take refuge. He is my shield and the horn of my salvation, my stronghold" (Ps. 18:1-2)? Was it excessive for another psalmist to declare, "God is our refuge and strength, an ever-present help in trouble" (Ps. 46:1)? Not when they knew God to be omnipresent and omnipotent, though otherwise it might have been. Knowledge of God's greatness (and his omnipresence and omnipotence are aspects of his greatness) naturally produces great faith and great praise.

PREDESTINATION
GOD HAS A PURPOSE

"I have loved you," says the LORD.
"But you ask, 'How have you loved us?'
"Was not Esau Jacob's brother?" the LORD
says. "Yet I have loved Jacob,
but Esau I have hated. . . ."

MALACHI 1:2-3

✝ The forty and more writers who produced the sixty-six books of Scripture over something like fifteen hundred years saw themselves and their readers as caught up in the outworking of God's sovereign purpose for his world, the purpose that led him to create, that sin then disrupted, and that his work of redemption is currently restoring. That purpose in essence was, and is, the endless expression and enjoyment of love between God and his rational creatures—love shown in their worship, praise, thanks, honor, glory, and service given to him, and in the fellowship, privileges, joys, and gifts that he gives to them.

The writers look back at what has already been done to advance God's redemptive plan for sin-damaged planet earth, and they look ahead to the day of its completion, when planet earth will be re-created in unimaginable glory (Isa. 65:17-25; 2 Pet. 3:10-13; Rev. 21:1–22:5). They proclaim God as the almighty Creator-Redeemer and dwell constantly on the multifaceted works of grace that God performs in history to secure for himself a people, a great company of individuals together, with whom his original purpose of giving and receiving love can be fulfilled. And the writers insist that as God has shown himself absolutely in control in bringing his plan to the point it has reached as they write, so he will continue in total control, working out everything according to his own will and so completing his redemptive project. It is within this frame of reference (Eph. 1:9-14; 2:4-10; 3:8-11; 4:11-16) that questions about predestination belong.

Predestination is a word often used to signify God's foreordaining of all the events of world history, past, present, and future, and this usage is quite appropriate. In Scripture and mainstream theology, however, predestination means specifically God's decision, made in eternity before the world and its inhabitants existed, regarding the final destiny of individual sinners. In fact, the New Testament uses the words predestination and election (the two are one), only of God's choice of particular sinners for salvation and eternal life (Rom. 8:29; Eph. 1:4-5, 11). Many have pointed out, however, that Scripture also ascribes to God an advance decision about those who finally are not saved (Rom. 9:6-29; 1 Pet. 2:8; Jude 4), and so it has become usual in Protestant theology to define God's predestination as including both his decision to save some from sin (election) and his decision to condemn the rest for their sin (reprobation), side by side.

To the question, "On what basis did God choose individuals for salvation?" it is sometimes replied: on the basis of his foreknowledge that when faced with the gospel they would choose Christ as their Savior. In that reply, foreknowledge means passive foresight on God's part of what individuals are going to do, without his predetermining their action. But

(a) *Foreknow* in Romans 8:29; 11:2 (cf. 1 Pet. 1:2 and 1:20, where the NIV renders the Greek *foreknown* as "chosen") means "fore-love" and "fore-appoint": it does not express the idea of a spectator's anticipation of what will spontaneously happen.

(b) Since all are naturally dead in sin (i.e., cut off from the life of God and unresponsive to him), no one who hears the gospel will ever come to repentance and faith without an inner quickening that only God can impart (Eph. 2:4-10). Jesus said: "No one can come to me unless the Father has enabled him" (John 6:65, cf. 44; 10:25-28). Sinners choose Christ only because God chose them for this choice and moved them to it by renewing their hearts.

Though all human acts are free in the sense of being self-determined, none are free from God's control according to his eternal purpose and foreordination.

Christians should therefore thank God for their conversion, look to him to keep them in the grace into which he has brought them, and confidently await his final triumph, according to his plan.

TRINITY

GOD IS ONE AND THREE

"This is what the LORD says—
Israel's King and Redeemer, the LORD
Almighty: I am the first and I am the last;
apart from me there is no God."

ISAIAH 44:6

✚ The Old Testament constantly insists that there is only one God, the self-revealed Creator, who must be worshiped and loved exclusively (Deut. 6:4-5; Isa. 44:6– 45:25). The New Testament agrees (Mark 12:29-30; 1 Cor. 8:4; Eph. 4:6; 1 Tim. 2:5) but speaks of three personal agents, Father, Son, and Holy Spirit, working together in the manner of a team to bring about salvation (Rom. 8; Eph. 1:3-14; 2 Thess. 2:13-14; 1 Pet. 1:2). The historic formulation of the Trinity (derived from the Latin word *trinitas*, meaning "threeness") seeks to circumscribe and safeguard this mystery (not explain it; that is beyond us), and it confronts us with perhaps the most difficult thought that the human mind has ever been asked to handle. It is not easy; but it is true.

The doctrine springs from the facts that the New Testament historians report, and from the revelatory teaching that, humanly speaking, grew out of these facts. Jesus, who prayed to his Father and taught his disciples to do the same, convinced them that he was personally divine, and belief in his divinity and in the rightness of offering him worship and prayer is basic to New Testament faith (John 20:28-31; cf. 1:18; Acts 7:59; Rom. 9:5; 10:9-13; 2 Cor. 12:7-9; Phil. 2:5-6; Col. 1:15-17; 2:9; Heb. 1:1-12; 1 Pet. 3:15). Jesus promised to send another Paraclete (he himself having been the first one), and *Paraclete* signifies a many-sided personal ministry as counselor, advocate, helper, comforter, ally, supporter (John 14:16-17, 26; 15:26-27; 16:7-15). This other Paraclete, who came at Pentecost to fulfill this promised ministry, was the Holy Spirit, recognized from the start as a third divine person: to lie to him, said Peter not long after Pentecost, is to lie to God (Acts 5:3-4).

So Christ prescribed baptism "in the name (singular: one God, one name) of the Father and of the Son and of the Holy Spirit"—the three persons who are the one God to whom Christians commit themselves (Matt. 28:19). So we meet the three persons in the account of Jesus' own baptism: the Father acknowledged the Son, and the Spirit showed his presence in the Son's life and ministry (Mark 1:9-11). So we read the trinitarian blessing of 2 Corinthians 13:14, and the prayer for grace and peace from the Father, the Spirit, and Jesus Christ in Revelation 1:4-5 (would John have put the Spirit between the Father and the Son if he had not regarded the Spirit as divine in the same sense as they are?). These are some of the more striking examples of the trinitarian outlook and emphasis of the New Testament. Though the technical language of historic trinitarianism is not found there, trinitarian faith and thinking are present throughout its pages, and in that sense the Trinity must be acknowledged as a biblical doctrine: an eternal truth about God which, though never explicit in the Old Testament, is plain and clear in the New.

The basic assertion of this doctrine is that the unity of the one God is complex. The three personal "subsistences" (as they are called) are coequal and coeternal centers of self-awareness, each being "I" in relation to two who are "you" and each partaking of the full divine essence (the "stuff" of deity, if we may dare to call it that) along with the other two. They are not three roles played by one person (that is *modalism*), nor are they three gods in a cluster (that is *tritheism*); the one God ("he") is also, and equally, "they," and "they" are always together and always cooperating, with the Father initiating, the Son complying, and the Spirit executing the will of both, which is his will also. This is the truth about God that was revealed through the words and works of Jesus, and that undergirds the reality of salvation as the New Testament sets it forth.

The practical importance of the doctrine of the Trinity is that it requires us to pay equal attention, and give equal honor, to all three persons in the unity of their gracious ministry to us. That ministry is the subject matter of the gospel, which, as Jesus' conversation with Nicodemus shows, cannot be stated without bringing in their distinct roles in God's plan of grace (John 3:1-15; note especially vv. 3, 5-8, 13-15, and John's expository comments, which NIV renders as part of the conversation itself, vv. 16-21). All non-Trinitarian formulations of the Christian message are by biblical standards inadequate and indeed fundamentally false, and will naturally tend to pull Christian lives out of shape.

HOLINESS

GOD IS LIGHT

*I am the LORD your God; consecrate
yourselves and be holy, because I am holy. . . .*

LEVITICUS 11:44

✝ When Scripture calls God, or individual persons of
the Godhead, "holy" (as it often does: Lev. 11:44-
45; Josh. 24:19; Isa. 2:2; Ps. 99:9; Isa. 1:4; 6:3; 41:14, 16,
20; 57:15; Ezek. 39:7; Amos 4:2; John 17:11; Acts 5:3-4,
32; Rev. 15:4), the word signifies everything about God
that sets him apart from us and makes him an object of
awe, adoration, and dread to us. It covers all aspects of his
transcendent greatness and moral perfection and thus is an
attribute of all his attributes, pointing to the "Godness" of
God at every point. Every facet of God's nature and every
aspect of his character may properly be spoken of as holy,
just because it is his. The core of the concept, however, is
God's purity, which cannot tolerate any form of sin (Hab.
1:13) and thus calls sinners to constant self-abasement in
his presence (Isa. 6:5).

Justice, which means doing in all circumstances things
that are right, is one expression of God's holiness. God
displays his justice as legislator and judge, and also as
promise-keeper and pardoner of sin. His moral law, requiring behavior that matches his own, is "holy, righteous

43

and good" (Rom. 7:12). He judges justly, according to actual desert (Gen. 18:25; Pss. 7:11; 96:13; Acts 17:31). His "wrath," that is, his active judicial hostility to sin, is wholly just in its manifestations (Rom. 2:5-16), and his particular "judgments" (retributive punishments) are glorious and praiseworthy (Rev. 16:5, 7; 19:1-4). Whenever God fulfills his covenant commitment by acting to save his people, it is a gesture of "righteousness," that is, justice (Isa. 51:5-6; 56:1; 63:1; 1 John 1:9). When God justifies sinners through faith in Christ, he does so on the basis of justice done, that is, the punishment of our sins in the person of Christ our substitute; thus the form taken by his justifying mercy shows him to be utterly and totally just (Rom. 3:25-26), and our justification itself is shown to be judicially justified.

When John says that God is "light," with no darkness in him at all, the image is affirming God's holy purity, which makes fellowship between him and the willfully unholy impossible and requires the pursuit of holiness and righteousness of life to be a central concern for Christian people (1 John 1:5–2:1; 2 Cor. 6:14–7:1; Heb. 12:10-17). The summons to believers, regenerate and forgiven as they are, to practice a holiness that will match God's own, and so please him, is constant in the New Testament, as indeed it was in the Old Testament (Deut. 30:1-10; Eph. 4:17–5:14; 1 Pet. 1:13-22). Because God is holy, God's people must be holy too.

GOODNESS

GOD IS LOVE

Give thanks to the LORD, for he is good. His love endures forever.

PSALM 136:1

✝ The statement "God is love" is often explained in terms of (a) the revelation, given through the life and teaching of Christ, of the endless life of the triune God as one of mutual affection and honor (Matt. 3:17; 17:5; John 3:35; 14:31; 16:13-14; 17:1-5, 22-26), linked with (b) the recognition that God made angels and humans to glorify their Maker in sharing the joyful give-and-take of this divine life according to their own creaturely mode. But, true as this seems to be, when John says "God is love" (1 John 4:8), what he means (as he goes on to explain) is that the Father through Christ has actually saved us formerly lost sinners who now believe. "This is how God showed his love among us: He sent his one and only Son into the world that we might live through him. This is love: not that we loved God"—we didn't—"but that he loved us and sent his Son as an atoning sacrifice for our sins" (vv. 9-10).

As always in the New Testament, "us" as the objects and beneficiaries of redeeming love means "us who believe." Neither here nor elsewhere does "we" or "us" refer to every individual belonging to the human race. New Testament teaching on redemption is particularistic throughout, and when "the world" is said to be loved and redeemed (John 3:16-17; 2 Cor. 5:19; 1 John 2:2), the reference is to the great number of God's elect scattered worldwide throughout the ungodly human community (cf. John 10:16; 11:52-53), not to each and every person who did, does, or shall exist. If this were not so, John and Paul would be contradicting things that they say elsewhere.

This sovereign redemptive love is one facet of the quality that Scripture calls God's goodness (Ps. 100:5; Mark 10:18), that is, the glorious kindness and generosity that touches all his creatures (Ps. 145:9, 15-16) and that ought to lead all sinners to repentance (Rom. 2:4). Other aspects of this goodness are the mercy or compassion or pity that shows kindness to persons in distress by rescuing them out of trouble (Pss. 107, 136) and the long-suffering, forbearance, and slowness to anger that continues to show kindness toward persons who have persisted in sinning (Exod. 34:6; Ps. 78:38; John 3:10–4:11; Rom. 9:22; 2 Pet. 3:9). The supreme expression of God's goodness is still, however, the amazing grace and inexpressible love that shows kindness by saving sinners who deserve only condemnation: saving them, moreover, at the tremendous cost of Christ's death on Calvary (Rom. 3:22-24; 5:5-8; 8:32-39; Eph. 2:1-10; 3:14-18; 5:25-27).

God's faithfulness to his purposes, promises, and people is a further aspect of his goodness and praiseworthiness. Humans lie and break their word; God does neither. In the worst of times it can still be said: "His compassions never fail. . . . Great is your faithfulness" (Lam. 3:22-23; Ps.

36:5; cf. Ps. 89, especially vv. 1-2, 14, 24, 33, 37, 49). Though God's ways of expressing his faithfulness are sometimes unexpected and bewildering, looking indeed to the casual observer and in the short term more like unfaithfulness, the final testimony of those who walk with God through life's ups and downs is that "every promise has been fulfilled; not one has failed" (Josh. 23:14-15). God's fidelity, along with the other aspects of his gracious goodness as set forth in his Word, is always solid ground on which to rest our faith and hope.

WISDOM

GOD'S TWOFOLD WILL IS ONE

*. . . Praise be to the name of God for ever
and ever; wisdom and power are his.*

DANIEL 2:20

✝ Wisdom in Scripture means choosing the best and noblest end at which to aim, along with the most appropriate and effective means to it. Human wisdom is displayed in the Old Testament Wisdom books (Job, Psalms, Proverbs, Ecclesiastes, and Song of Songs, showing how to suffer, pray, live, enjoy, and love, respectively) and in James's letter (enforcing consistent Christian behavior): it means making the "fear" of God—that is, reverent worship and service of him—one's goal (Prov. 1:7; 9:10; Eccles. 12:13) and cultivating prudence, fortitude, forbearance, and zeal as means to it. God's wisdom is seen in his works of creation, preservation, and redemption: it is his choice of his own glory as his goal (Ps. 46:10; Isa. 42:8; 48:11), and his decision to achieve it first by creating a marvelous variety of things and people (Ps. 104:24; Prov. 3:19-20), second by kindly providences of all sorts (Ps. 145:13-16; Acts 14:17), and third by the redemptive "wisdom" of "Christ crucified" (1 Cor. 1:18–2:16) and the resultant world church (Eph. 3:10).

The outworking of God's wisdom involves the expression of his will in both senses that that phrase bears. In the first and fundamental sense, God's will is his decision, or decree, about what shall happen—"his eternal purpose, according to the counsel of his will, whereby, for his own glory, he hath foreordained whatsoever comes to pass" (Westminster Shorter Catechism Q.7). This is God's will of events, referred to in Ephesians 1:11. In the second and secondary sense, the will of God is his command, that is, his instruction, given in Scripture, as to how people should and should not behave: it is sometimes called his will of precept (see Rom. 12:2; Eph. 5:17; Col. 1:9; 1 Thess. 4:3-6). Some of its requirements are rooted in his holy character, which we are to imitate: such are the principles of the Decalogue and the two great commandments (Exod. 20:1-17; Matt. 22:37-40; cf. Eph. 4:32–5:2). Some of its requirements spring simply from the divine institution: such were circumcision and the Old Testament sacrificial and purity laws, and such are baptism and the Lord's Supper today. But all bind the conscience alike, and God's plan of events already includes the "good works" of obedience that those who believe will perform (Eph. 2:10).

It is sometimes hard to believe that costly obedience, putting us at a disadvantage in the world (as loyal obedience to God often does), is part of a predestined plan for furthering both God's glory and our own good (Rom. 8:28). But we are to glorify God by believing that it is so, and that one day we shall see it to be so; for his wisdom is supreme and never fails. Making known his will of precept, and governing the responses of human free agency to it, is one means whereby God accomplishes his will of events, even when the response is one of unbelief and disobedience. Paul illustrates this when he tells the Romans that Israel's unbelief has its place in God's plan for advancing the gospel (Rom. 11:11-15, 25-32): a realization that prompts the cry: "Oh, the depth of the riches of the wisdom . . . of God! . . . To him be the glory for ever! Amen" (vv. 33, 36). Let that be our cry too.

MYSTERY

GOD IS SURPASSINGLY GREAT

Yours, O LORD, is the greatness and the
power and the glory and the majesty and the
splendor, for everything in heaven and earth
is yours. Yours, O LORD, is the kingdom;
you are exalted as head over all.

1 CHRONICLES 29:11

✝ God is great, says Scripture (Deut. 7:21; Neh. 4:14; Pss. 48:1; 86:10; 95:3; 145:3; Dan. 9:4): greater than we can grasp. Theology states this by describing him as incomprehensible—not in the sense that logic is somehow different for him from what it is for us, so that we cannot follow the workings of his mind at all, but in the sense that we can never understand him fully, just because he is infinite and we are finite. Scripture pictures God as dwelling not only in thick and impenetrable darkness but also in unapproachable light (Ps. 97:2; 1 Tim. 6:16), and both images express the same thought: our Creator is above us, and it is beyond our power to take his measure in any way.

This is sometimes expressed by speaking of the mystery of God, using that word not in the biblical sense of a secret that God has now revealed (Dan. 2:29-30; Eph. 3:2-6) but in the more recently developed sense of a reality that we lack the capacity to understand properly, no matter how much is said about it. God tells us in the Bible that creation, providential government, the Trinity, the Incarnation, the regenerating work of the Spirit, union with Christ in his death and resurrection, and the inspiration of Scripture—to go no further—are facts, and we take his word for it that they are; but we believe that they are without knowing how they can be. As creatures, we are unable fully to comprehend either the being or the actions of the Creator.

As it would be wrong, however, to suppose ourselves to know everything about God (and so in effect to imprison him in the box of our own limited notion of him), so it would be wrong to doubt whether our concept constitutes real knowledge of him. Part of the significance of our creation in God's image is that we are able both to know about him and to know him relationally in a true if limited sense of "know"; and what God tells us in Scripture about himself is true as far as it goes. Calvin spoke of God as having condescended to our weakness and accommodated himself to our capacity, both in the inspiring of the Scriptures and in the incarnating of the Son, so that he might give us genuine understanding of himself. The form and substance of a parent's baby talk bears no comparison with the full contents of that parent's mind, which he or she could express in full if talking to another adult; but the child receives from the baby talk factual information, real if limited, about the parent, and responsive love and trust grow accordingly. That is the analogy here.

Now we see why our Creator presents himself to us anthropomorphically, as having a face (Exod. 33:11), a hand (1 Sam. 5:11), an arm (Isa. 53:1), ears (Neh. 1:6), eyes (Job 28:10), and feet (Nah. 1:3), and as sitting on a throne (1 Kings 22:19), flying on the wind (Ps. 18:10), and fighting in battle (2 Chron. 32:8; Isa. 63:1-6). These are not descriptions of what God is in himself but of what he is to us: namely, the transcendent Lord who relates to his people as Father and friend, and acts as their ally. God sets himself before us in this way to draw us out in worship, love, and trust, even though conceptually we are always like the young children who hear their parents' baby talk and know the talker only in part (1 Cor. 13:12).

We should never forget that in any case theology is for doxology: the truest expression of trust in a great God will always be worship, and it will always be proper worship to praise God for being far greater than we can know.

PROVIDENCE
GOD GOVERNS THIS WORLD

*The lot is cast into the lap, but its every
decision is from the LORD.*

PROVERBS 16:33

✝ "God's works of providence are his most holy, wise, and powerful preserving and governing all his creatures, and all their actions" (Westminster Shorter Catechism Q.11). If Creation was a unique exercise of divine energy causing the world to be, providence is a continued exercise of that same energy whereby the Creator, according to his own will, (a) keeps all creatures in being, (b) involves himself in all events, and (c) directs all things to their appointed end. The model is of purposive personal management with total "hands-on" control: God is completely in charge of his world. His hand may be hidden, but his rule is absolute.

Some have restricted God's providence to foreknowledge without control, or upholding without intervention, or general oversight without concern for details, but the testimony to providence as formulated above is overwhelming.

The Bible clearly teaches God's providential control (1) over the universe at large, Ps. 103:19; Dan. 4:35; Eph. 1:11; (2) over the physical world, Job 37; Pss. 104:14; 135:6;

Matt. 5:45; (3) over the brute creation, Ps. 104:21, 28; Matt. 6:26; 10:29; (4) over the affairs of nations, Job 12:23; Pss. 22:28; 66:7; Acts 17:26; (5) over man's birth and lot in life, 1 Sam. 16:1; Ps. 139:16; Isa. 45:5; Gal. 1:15-16; (6) over the outward successes and failures of men's lives, Ps. 75:6, 7; Luke 1:52; (7) over things seemingly accidental or insignificant, Prov. 16:33; Matt. 10:30; (8) in the protection of the righteous, Pss. 4:8; 5:12; 63:8; 121:3; Rom. 8:28; (9) in supplying the wants of God's people, Gen. 22:8, 14; Deut. 8:3; Phil. 4:19; (10) in giving answers to prayer, 1 Sam. 1:19; Isa. 20:5, 6; 2 Chron. 33:13; Ps. 65:2; Matt. 7:7; Luke 18:7, 8; and (11) in the exposure and punishment of the wicked, Pss. 7:12-13; 11:6. (L. Berkhof, Systematic Theology, 4th ed.)

Clear thinking about God's involvement in the world-process and in the acts of rational creatures requires complementary sets of statements, thus: a person takes action, or an event is triggered by natural causes, or Satan shows his hand—yet God overrules. This is the message of the book of Esther, where God's name nowhere appears. Again: things that are done contravene God's will of command—yet they fulfill his will of events (Eph. 1:11). Again: humans mean what they do for evil—yet God who overrules uses their actions for good (Gen. 50:20; Acts 2:23). Again: humans, under God's overruling, sin—yet God is not the author of sin (James 1:13-17); rather, he is its judge.

The nature of God's "concurrent" or "confluent" involvement in all that occurs in his world, as—without violating the nature of things, the ongoing causal processes, or human free agency—he makes his will of events come to pass, is mystery to us, but the consistent biblical teaching about God's involvement is as stated above.

Of the evils that infect God's world (moral and spiritual perversity, waste of good, and the physical disorders and disruptions of a spoiled cosmos), it can summarily be said: God permits evil (Acts 14:16); he punishes evil with evil (Ps. 81:11-12; Rom. 1:26-32); he brings good out of evil (Gen. 50:20; Acts 2:23; 4:27-28; 13:27; 1 Cor. 2:7-8); he uses evil to test and discipline those he loves (Matt. 4:1-11; Heb. 12:4-14); and one day he will redeem his people from the power and presence of evil altogether (Rev. 21:27; 22:14-15).

The doctrine of providence teaches Christians that they are never in the grip of blind forces (fortune, chance, luck, fate); all that happens to them is divinely planned, and each event comes as a new summons to trust, obey, and rejoice, knowing that all is for one's spiritual and eternal good (Rom. 8:28).

MIRACLES

GOD SHOWS HIS PRESENCE AND POWER

The LORD heard Elijah's cry,
and the boy's life returned to him,
and he lived.

1 KINGS 17:22

✝ Scripture has no single word for miracle. The concept is a blend of the thoughts expressed by three terms: *wonder, mighty work,* and *sign.*

Wonder is the primary notion. (*Miracle,* from the Latin *miraculum,* means something that evokes wonder.) A miracle is an observed event that triggers awareness of God's presence and power. Striking providences and coincidences, and awesome events such as childbirth, no less than works of new creative power, are properly called miracles since they communicate this awareness. In this sense, at least, there are miracles today.

Mighty work (work of power) focuses on the impression that miracles make, and points to the presence in Bible history of supernatural acts of God involving the power that created the world from nothing. Thus, the raising of the dead to life, which Jesus did three times, not counting his own resurrection (Luke 7:11-17; 8:49-56; John 11:38-44), and Elijah, Elisha, Peter, and Paul did once each (1 Kings 17:17-24; 2 Kings 4:18-37; Acts 9:36-41; 20:9-

12), is a work of this creative power; it cannot be explained in terms of coincidence or of nature taking its course. The same is true of organic healings, of which the Gospels recount many; they too exhibit supernatural re-creating and restoring.

Sign as a label for miracles (the label regularly used in John's Gospel, where seven key miracles are recorded) means that they signify something; in other words, they carry a message. The miracles in Scripture are nearly all clustered in the time of the Exodus, of Elijah and Elisha, and of Christ and his apostles. First of all, they authenticate the miracle workers themselves as God's representatives and messengers (cf. Exod. 4:1-9; 1 Kings 17:24; John 10:38; 14:11; 2 Cor. 12:12; Heb. 2:3-4); and they also show forth something of God's power in salvation and judgment. Such is their significance.

Belief in the miraculous is integral to Christianity. Theologians who discard all miracles, thus obliging themselves to deny Jesus' incarnation and resurrection, the two supreme miracles of Scripture, should not claim to be Christians: the claim is not valid. The rejection of miracles by yesterday's scientists sprang not from science but from the dogma of a universe of absolute uniformity that scientists brought to their scientific work. There is nothing irrational about believing that God who made the world can still intrude creatively into it. Christians should recognize that it is not faith in the biblical miracles, and in God's ability to work miracles today should he so wish, but doubt about these things, that is unreasonable.

GLORY

GOD'S GLORY-SHOWING REQUIRES GLORY-GIVING

Like the appearance of a rainbow
in the clouds on a rainy day,
so was the radiance around him.

EZEKIEL 1:28

✝ God's goal is his glory, but this needs careful explanation, for it is easily misunderstood. It points to a purpose not of divine egoism, as is sometimes imagined, but of divine love. Certainly, God wants to be praised for his praiseworthiness and exalted for his greatness and goodness; he wants to be appreciated for what he is. But the glory that is his goal is in fact a two-sided, two-stage relationship: it is, precisely, a conjunction of (a) revelatory acts on his part whereby he shows his glory to men and angels in free generosity, with (b) responsive adoration on their part whereby they give him glory out of gratitude for what they have seen and received. In this conjunction is realized the fellowship of love for which God's rational creatures were and are made, and for which fallen human beings have now been redeemed. The to-and-fro of seeing glory in God and giving glory to God is the true fulfillment of human nature at its heart, and it brings supreme joy to man just as it does to God (cf. Zeph. 3:14-17).

"Glory" in the Old Testament carries associations of

59

weight, worth, wealth, splendor, and dignity, all of which are present when God is said to have revealed his glory. God was answering Moses' plea to be shown God's glory when he proclaimed to Moses his name (i.e., his nature, character, and power, Exod. 33:18–34:7). With that proclamation went an awe-inspiring physical manifestation, the Shekinah, a bright shining cloud that could look like fire, white-hot (Exod. 24:17). The Shekinah was itself called the glory of God; it appeared at significant moments in the Bible story as a sign of God's active presence (Exod. 33:22; 34:5; cf. 16:7, 10; 24:15-17; 40:34-35; Lev. 9:23-24; 1 Kings 8:10-11; Ezek. 1:28; 8:4; 9:3; 10:4; 11:22-23; Matt. 17:5; Luke 2:9; cf. Acts 1:9; 1 Thess. 4:17; Rev. 1:7). New Testament writers proclaim that the glory of God's nature, character, power, and purpose is now open to view in the person and role of God's incarnate Son, Jesus Christ (John 1:14-18; 2 Cor. 4:3-6; Heb. 1:1-3).

God's glory, shown forth in the plan and work of grace whereby he saves sinners, is meant to call forth praise (Eph. 1:6, 12, 14), that is, the giving of glory to God by spoken words (cf. Rev. 4:9; 19:7). All life activities, too, must be pursued with the aim of giving God homage, honor, and pleasure, which is glory-giving on the practical level (1 Cor. 10:31).

God would not share with idols the praise for restoring his people, for idols, being unreal, contributed nothing to this work of grace (Isa. 42:8; 48:11); and God will not share the praise for salvation with its human subjects today, for we too contribute nothing more to it than our need of it. First to last, and at every stage in the process, salvation comes from the Lord, and our praise must show our awareness of that. This is why Reformation theology was so insistent on the principle, "Glory to God *alone*" (*soli Deo gloria*), and why we need to maintain that principle with equal zeal today.

IDOLATRY
GOD DEMANDS TOTAL ALLEGIANCE

"I will punish her for the days she burned
incense to the Baals; she decked herself with
rings and jewelry, and went after her lovers,
but me she forgot," declares the LORD.

HOSEA 2:13

✝ Though there is only one God and only one true faith, namely that taught in the Bible, our apostate world (Rom. 1:18-25) has always been full of religions, and the age-old urging toward syncretism, whereby aspects of one religion are assimilated into another thus changing both, is still with us. Indeed, it has been startlingly revived in our time through the renewed academic quest for a transcendent unity of religions and the flowering of the popular amalgam of Eastern and Western ideas that calls itself the New Age.

The pressure here is not new. Having occupied Canaan, Israel was constantly tempted to absorb Canaanite worship of fertility gods and goddesses into the worship of Yahweh, and to make images of Yahweh himself—both of which moves the law forbade (Exod. 20:3-6). The spiritual issue was whether the Israelites would remember that Yahweh, their covenant God, was all-sufficient for them, and moreover claimed their exclusive allegiance, so that worshiping other gods was spiritual adultery (Jer. 3; Ezek. 16; Hos. 2). This was a test the nation largely failed.

Syncretism was similarly widespread and approved in the first-century Roman empire, where polytheism was rife and all sorts of cults flourished. Christian teachers fought hard to keep the faith from being assimilated to Gnosticism (a kind of theosophy that had no use for incarnation and atonement, since it saw man's problem as one of ignorance, not sin), and later to Neoplatonism and Manichaeism, both of which, like Gnosticism, saw salvation as mainly a matter of getting detached from the physical world. These conflicts were relatively successful, and the classic creedal formulations of the Trinity and the Incarnation are part of their permanent legacy.

Scripture is stern about the evil of practicing idolatry. Idols are mocked as delusive nonentities (Ps. 115:4-7; Isa. 44:9-20), but they enslave their worshippers in blind superstition (Isa. 44:20) which is infidelity towards God (Jer. 2), and Paul adds that demons operate through idols, making them a positive spiritual menace, contact with which cannot but corrupt (1 Cor. 8:4-6; 10:19-21). In our post-Christian Western culture, which is prepared to fill the spiritual vacuum that people feel by looking kindly on syncretism, witchcraft, and experiments with the occult, the biblical warnings against idolatry need to be taken to heart (cf. 1 Cor. 10:14; 1 John 5:19-21).

ANGELS

GOD EMPLOYS
SUPERNATURAL AGENTS

I asked, "What are these, my lord?"
The angel who was talking with me
answered, "I will show you what they are."
Then the man standing among the myrtle
trees explained, "They are the ones the LORD
has sent to go throughout the earth."

ZECHARIAH 1:9-10

✝ Angels (their name means "messengers") are one of the two sorts of personal beings that God created, humankind being the other. There are many of them (Matt. 26:53; Rev. 5:11). They are intelligent moral agents, not embodied or ordinarily visible, although they are able to show themselves to humans in what appears as a physical form (Gen. 18:2–19:22; John 20:10-14; Acts 12:7-10). They do not marry, and they are not subject to death (Matt. 22:30; Luke 20:35-36). They can move from one point in space to another, and many of them can congregate in a tiny area (Luke 8:30, where the reference is to fallen angels).

Like human beings, the angels were originally set under probation, and some of them fell into sin. The many who passed the test are now evidently confirmed in a state of holiness and immortal glory. Heaven is their headquarters

(Matt. 18:10; 22:30; Rev. 5:11), where they constantly worship God (Pss. 103:20-21; 148:2) and whence they move out to render service to Christians at God's bidding (Heb. 1:14). These are the "holy" and "elect" angels (Matt. 25:31; Mark 8:38; Luke 9:26; Acts 10:22; 1 Tim. 5:21; Rev. 14:10), to whom God's work of grace through Christ is currently demonstrating more of the divine wisdom and glory than they knew before (Eph. 3:10; 1 Pet. 1:12).

Holy angels guard believers (Pss. 34:7; 91:11), little ones in particular (Matt. 18:10), and constantly observe what goes on in the church (1 Cor. 11:10). It is implied that they are more knowledgeable about divine things than humans are (Mark 13:32), and that they have a special ministry to believers at the time of their death (Luke 16:22), but we know no details about any of this. Suffice it to pinpoint the relevance of angels by saying that if at any time we stand in need of their ministry, we shall receive it; and that as the world watches Christians in hope of seeing them tumble, so do good angels watch Christians in hope of seeing grace triumph in their lives.

The mysterious "angel of the LORD" or "angel of God," who appears often in the early Old Testament story and is sometimes identified with the God from whom he is at other times distinguished (Gen. 16:7-13; 18:1-33; 22:11-18; 24:7, 40; 31:11-13; 32:24-30; 48:15-16; Exod. 3:2-6; 14:19; 23:20-23; 32:34–33:5; Num. 22:22-35; Josh. 5:13-15; Judg. 2:1-5; 6:11-23; 9:13-23), is in some sense God acting as his own messenger, and is commonly seen as a preincarnate appearance of God the Son.

Angelic activity was prominent at the great turning points in the divine plan of salvation (the days of the patriarchs, the time of the Exodus and giving of the law, the period of the Exile and restoration, and the birth, resurrection, and ascension of Jesus Christ), and it will be prominent again when Christ returns (Matt. 25:31; Mark 8:38).

DEMONS

GOD HAS SUPERNATURAL
OPPONENTS

*They sacrificed to demons,
which are not God—
gods they had not known,
gods that recently appeared,
gods your fathers did not fear.*

DEUTERONOMY 32:17

✝ "Demon," or "devil" as earlier translations rendered the words, is the Greek *daimon* and *daimonion*, the regular terms in the Gospels for the spiritual beings, corrupt and hostile to both God and man, whom Jesus exorcised from their victims in large numbers during his earthly ministry. The demons were fallen angels, deathless creatures serving Satan (Jesus equated Beelzebub, their reputed prince, with Satan: Matt. 12:24-29). Having joined Satan's rebellion, they were cast out of heaven to await final judgment (2 Pet. 2:4; Jude 6). Their minds are permanently set to oppose God, goodness, truth, the kingdom of Christ, and the welfare of human beings, and they have real if limited power and freedom of movement, though in Calvin's picturesque phrase they drag their chains wherever they go and can never hope to overcome God.

The level and intensity of demonic manifestations in people during Christ's ministry was unique, having no parallel in Old Testament times or since; it was doubtless part of Satan's desperate battle for his kingdom against Christ's attack on it (Matt. 12:29). Demons were revealed as having knowledge and strength (Mark 1:24; 9:17-27). They inflicted, or at least exploited, physical and mental maladies (Mark 5:1-15; 9:17-18; Luke 11:14). They recognized and feared Christ, to whose authority they were subject (Mark 1:25; 3:11-12; 9:25), though by his own confession it was only through effort in prayer that he was able to expel them (Mark 9:29).

Christ authorized and equipped the Twelve and the seventy to exorcise in his name (i.e., by his power—Luke 9:1; 10:17), and the ministry of exorcism continues still as an occasional pastoral necessity. The sixteenth-century Lutheran church abolished exorcism, believing that Christ's victory over Satan had suppressed demonic invasion forever, but this was premature.

Satan's army of demons uses subtler strategies also, namely, deception and discouragement in many forms. Opposing these is the essence of spiritual warfare (Eph. 6:10-18). Though demons can give trouble of many kinds to regenerate persons in whom the Holy Spirit dwells, they cannot finally thwart God's purpose of saving his elect any more than they can finally avoid their own eternal torment. As the devil is God's devil (that is Luther's phrase), so the demons are God's demons, defeated enemies (Col. 2:15) whose limited power is prolonged only for the advancement of God's glory as his people contend with them.

SATAN

FALLEN ANGELS HAVE A LEADER

One day the angels came to present
themselves before the LORD,
and Satan also came with them.

JOB 1:6

✝ Satan, leader of the fallen angels, comes like them into full view only in the New Testament. His name means "adversary" (opponent of God and his people), and the Old Testament introduces him as such (1 Chron. 21:1; Job 1-2; Zech. 3:1-2). The New Testament gives him revealing titles: "devil" (*diabolos*) means accuser (i.e., of God's people: Rev. 12:9-10); "Apollyon" (Rev. 9:11) means destroyer; "the tempter" (Matt. 4:3; 1 Thess. 3:5) and "the evil one" (1 John 5:18-19) mean what they say; "prince" and "god of this world" point to Satan as presiding over mankind's anti-God life-styles (John 12:31; 14:30; 16:11; 2 Cor. 4:4; cf. Eph. 2:2; 1 John 5:19; Rev. 12:9). Jesus said that Satan was always a murderer and is the father of lies—that is, he is both the original liar and the sponsor of all subsequent falsehood and deceits (John 8:44). Finally, he is identified as the serpent who fooled Eve in Eden (Rev. 12:9; 20:2). The picture is one of unimaginable meanness, malice, fury, and cruelty directed against God, against God's truth, and against those to whom God has extended his saving love.

Satan's deceptive cunning is highlighted by Paul's statement that he becomes an angel of light, disguising evil as good (2 Cor. 11:14). His destructive ferocity comes out in the description of him as a roaring, devouring lion (1 Pet. 5:8) and as a dragon (Rev. 12:9). As he was Christ's sworn foe (Matt. 4:1-11; 16:23; Luke 4:13; John 14:30; cf. Luke 22:3, 53), so now he is the Christian's, always probing for weaknesses, misdirecting strengths, and undermining faith, hope, and character (Luke 22:32; 2 Cor. 2:11; 11:3-15; Eph. 6:16). He should be taken seriously, for malice and cunning make him fearsome; yet not so seriously as to provoke abject terror of him, for he is a beaten enemy. Satan is stronger than we are, but Christ has triumphed over Satan (Matt. 12:29), and Christians will triumph over him too if they resist him with the resources that Christ supplies (Eph. 6:10-13; James 4:7; 1 Pet. 5:9-10). "The one who is in you is greater than the one who is in the world" (1 John 4:4).

Acknowledging Satan's reality, taking his opposition seriously, noting his strategy (anything, provided it be not biblical Christianity), and reckoning on always being at war with him—this is not a lapse into a dualistic concept of two gods, one good, one evil, fighting it out. Satan is a creature, superhuman but not divine; he has much knowledge and power, but he is neither omniscient nor omnipotent; he can move around in ways that humans cannot, but he is not omnipresent; and he is an already defeated rebel, having no more power than God allows him and being destined for the lake of fire (Rev. 20:10).

HUMANNESS

GOD MADE HUMAN BEINGS
IN HIS IMAGE

So God created man in his own image,
in the image of God he created him;
male and female he created them.

GENESIS 1:27

✝ The statement at the start of the Bible (Gen. 1:26-27, echoed in 5:1; 9:6; 1 Cor. 11:7; James 3:9) that God made man in his own image, so that humans are like God as no other earthly creatures are, tells us that the special dignity of being human is that, as humans, we may reflect and reproduce at our own creaturely level the holy ways of God, and thus act as his direct representatives on earth. This is what humans are made to do, and in one sense we are human only to the extent that we are doing it.

The scope of God's image in man is not defined in Genesis 1:26-27, but the context makes it clear. Genesis 1:1-25 sets forth God as personal, rational (having intelligence and will, able to form plans and execute them), creative competent to control the world he has made, and morally admirable, in that all he creates is good. Plainly, God's image will include all these qualities. Verses 28-30 show God blessing newly created humans (that must mean telling them their privilege and destiny) and setting them

71

to rule creation as his representatives and deputies. The human capacity for communication and relationship with both God and other humans, and the God-given dominion over the lower creation (highlighted in Ps. 8 as the answer to the question, What is man?), thus appear as further facets of the image.

God's image in man at Creation, then, consisted (a) in man's being a "soul" or "spirit" (Gen. 2:7, where the NIV correctly says "living being"; Eccles. 12:7), that is, a personal, self-conscious, Godlike creature with a Godlike capacity for knowledge, thought, and action; (b) in man's being morally upright, a quality lost at the Fall that is now being progressively restored in Christ (Eph. 4:24; Col. 3:10); (c) in man's environmental dominion. Usually, and reasonably, it is added that (d) man's God-given immortality and (e) the human body, through which we experience reality, express ourselves, and exercise our dominion, belong to the image too.

The body belongs to the image, not directly, since God, as we noted earlier, does not have one, but indirectly, inasmuch as the God-like activities of exercising dominion over the material creation and demonstrating affection to other rational beings make our embodiment necessary. There is no fully human life without a functioning body, whether here or hereafter. That truth, implicit in Genesis 1, was made explicit by the incarnation and resurrection of Jesus Christ: as the true image of God in his humanity as well as in his divinity. The glorified Lord Jesus is embodied to all eternity, just as Christians will be.

The Fall diminished God's image not only in Adam and Eve but in all their descendants, that is, the whole human race. We retain the image structurally, in the sense that our humanity is intact, but not functionally, for we are now sin's slaves and unable to use our powers to mirror God's holiness. Regeneration begins the process of restoring God's moral image in our lives, but not till we are fully sanctified and glorified shall we reflect God perfectly in thought and action as mankind was made to do and as the incarnate Son of God in his humanity did and does (John 4:34; 5:30; 6:38; 8:29, 46; Rom. 6:4, 5, 10; 8:11).

HUMANKIND
HUMANS ARE BODY AND SOUL, IN TWO GENDERS

The LORD God formed the man from the dust of the ground and breathed into his nostrils the breath of life, and the man became a living being.

GENESIS 2:7

Male and female he created them.

GENESIS 1:27

✝ Each human being in this world consists of a material body animated by an immaterial personal self. Scripture calls this self a "soul" or "spirit." "Soul" emphasizes the distinctness of a person's conscious selfhood as such; "spirit" carries the nuances of the self's derivation from God, dependence on him, and distinctness from the body as such.

Biblical usage leads us to say that we *have* and *are* both souls and spirits, but it is a mistake to think that soul and spirit are two different things; a "trichotomous" view of man as body, soul, and spirit is incorrect. The common idea that the soul is an organ of this-worldly awareness only and that the spirit is a distinct organ of communion with God that is brought to life in regeneration is out of step with biblical teaching and word usage. Moreover, it leads to a crippling anti-intellectualism whereby spiritual insight and theological thought are separated to the impoverishing of both, theology being seen as "soulish" and unspiritual while spiritual perception is thought of as unrelated to the teaching and learning of God's revealed truth.

The embodiment of the soul is integral to God's design for mankind. Through the body, as was said earlier, we are to experience our environment, enjoy and control things around us, and relate to other people. There was nothing evil or corruptible about the body as God first made it, and had sin not come in, the physical ailing, aging, and rotting that leads to death as we know it would have been no part of human life (Gen. 2:17; 3:19, 22; Rom. 5:12). Now, however, human beings are corrupt throughout their psycho-physical being, as their disordered desires, both physical and mental, warring against each other as well as against the rules of wisdom and righteousness, clearly show.

At death the soul leaves the defunct body behind, but this is not the happy release that Greek philosophers and some cultists have imagined. The Christian hope is not redemption *from* the body but redemption *of* the body. We look forward to our participation in Christ's resurrection in and through the resurrection of our own bodies. Though the exact composition of our future glorified bodies is presently unknown, we know that there will be some sort of continuity with our present bodies (1 Cor. 15:35-49; Phil. 3:20-21; Col. 3:4).

The two genders, male and female, belong to the Creation pattern. Men and women are equally God's image-bearers (Gen. 1:27), and their dignity is equal in consequence. The complementary nature of the genders is meant to lead to enriching cooperation (see Gen. 2:18-

23) as their roles are fulfilled not just in marriage, procreation, and family life, but in life's wider activities also. Perception of the unfathomable difference between a person of the other gender and oneself is meant to be a school for learning the practice and joy of appreciation, openness, honor, service, and fidelity, all of which belong to the courtesy that the mysterious reality of the other gender requires. The ideology of "unisex," which plays down the significance of the two genders, thus perverts God's order, while the French tag on gender distinction, *"vive la différence!"* (Long live the contrast!) expresses the biblical viewpoint.

PART TWO
GOD REVEALED AS REDEEMER

THE FALL

THE FIRST HUMAN COUPLE SINNED

*When the woman saw that the fruit of the
tree was good for food and pleasing to the
eye, and also desirable for gaining wisdom,
she took some and ate it. She also gave some
to her husband, who was with her,
and he ate it.*

GENESIS 3:6

✠ Paul, in Romans, affirms that all mankind is naturally under the guilt and power of sin, the reign of
death, and the inescapable wrath of God (Rom. 3:9, 19;
5:17, 21; 1:18-19; cf. the whole section, 1:18–3:20). He
traces this back to the sin of the one man whom, when
speaking at Athens, he described as our common ancestor
(Rom. 5:12-14; Acts 17:26; cf. 1 Cor. 15:22). This is
authoritative apostolic interpretation of the history recorded in Genesis 3, where we find the account of the Fall,
the original human lapse from God and godliness into sin
and lostness. The main points in that history, as seen
through the lens of Paul's interpretation, are as follows:

(a) God made the first man the representative for all his
posterity, just as he was to make Jesus Christ the representative for all God's elect (Rom. 5:15-19 with 8:29-30;
9:22-26). In each case the representative was to involve
those whom he represented in the fruits of his personal

79

action, whether for good or ill, just as a national leader involves his people in the consequences of his action when, for instance, he declares war. This divinely chosen arrangement, whereby Adam would determine the destiny of his descendants, has been called the covenant of works, though this is not a biblical phrase.

(b) God set the first man in a state of happiness and promised to continue this to him and his posterity after him if he showed fidelity by a course of perfect positive obedience and specifically by not eating from a tree described as the tree of the knowledge of good and evil. It would seem that the tree bore this name because the issue was whether Adam would let God tell him what was good and bad for him or would seek to decide that for himself, in disregard of what God had said. By eating from this tree Adam would, in effect, be claiming that he could know and decide what was good and evil for him without any reference to God.

(c) Adam, led by Eve, who was herself led by the serpent (Satan in disguise: 2 Cor. 11:3 with v. 14; Rev. 12:9), defied God by eating the forbidden fruit. The results were that, first, the anti-God, self-aggrandizing mindset expressed in Adam's sin became part of him and of the moral nature that he passed on to his descendants (Gen. 6:5; Rom. 3:9-20). Second, Adam and Eve found themselves gripped by a sense of pollution and guilt that made them ashamed and fearful before God—with good reason. Third, they were cursed with expectations of pain and death, and they were expelled from Eden. At the same time, however, God began to show them saving mercy; he made them skin garments to cover their nakedness, and he promised that the woman's seed would one day break the serpent's head. This foreshadowed Christ.

Though telling the story in a somewhat figurative style, Genesis asks us to read it as history; in Genesis, Adam is linked to the patriarchs and with them to the rest of mankind by genealogy (chs. 5, 10, 11), which makes him as much a part of space-time history as were Abraham, Isaac, and Jacob. All the book's main characters after Adam, except Joseph, are shown as sinners in one way or another, and the death of Joseph, like the death of almost everyone else in the story, is carefully recorded (Gen. 50:22-26); Paul's statement "In Adam all die" (1 Cor. 15:22) only makes explicit what Genesis already clearly implies.

It may fairly be claimed that the Fall narrative gives the only convincing explanation of the perversity of human nature that the world has ever seen. Pascal said that the doctrine of original sin seems an offense to reason, but once accepted it makes total sense of the entire human condition. He was right, and the same thing may and should be said of the Fall narrative itself.

ORIGINAL SIN

DEPRAVITY INFECTS EVERYONE

Surely I was sinful at birth, sinful from the
time my mother conceived me.

PSALM 51:5

✝ Scripture diagnoses sin as a universal deformity of
human nature, found at every point in every person
(1 Kings 8:46; Rom. 3:9-23; 7:18; 1 John 1:8-10). Both
Testaments have names for it that display its ethical character as rebellion against God's rule, missing the mark
God set us to aim at, transgressing God's law, disobeying
God's directives, offending God's purity by defiling oneself, and incurring guilt before God the Judge. This moral
deformity is dynamic: sin stands revealed as an energy of
irrational, negative, and rebellious reaction to God's call
and command, a spirit of fighting God in order to play
God. The root of sin is pride and enmity against God, the
spirit seen in Adam's first transgression; and sinful acts
always have behind them thoughts, motives, and desires
that one way or another express the willful opposition of
the fallen heart to God's claims on our lives.

Sin may be comprehensively defined as lack of conformity to the law of God in act, habit, attitude, outlook,
disposition, motivation, and mode of existence. Scriptures
that illustrate different aspects of sin include Jeremiah

17:9; Matthew 12:30-37; Mark 7:20-23; Romans 1:18–3:20; 7:7-25; 8:5-8; 14:23 (Luther said that Paul wrote Romans to "magnify sin"); Galatians 5:16-21; Ephesians 2:1-3; 4:17-19; Hebrews 3:12; James 2:10-11; 1 John 3:4; 5:17. *Flesh* in Paul usually means a human being driven by sinful desire; the NIV renders these instances of the word as "sinful nature." The particular faults and vices (i.e., forms and expression of sin) that Scripture detects and denounces are too numerous to list here.

Original sin, meaning sin derived from our origin, is not a biblical phrase (Augustine coined it), but it is one that brings into fruitful focus the reality of sin in our spiritual system. The assertion of original sin means not that sin belongs to human nature as God made it (God made mankind upright, Eccles. 7:29), nor that sin is involved in the processes of reproduction and birth (the uncleanness connected with menstruation, semen, and childbirth in Leviticus 12 and 15 was typical and ceremonial only, not moral and real), but that (a) sinfulness marks everyone from birth, and is there in the form of a motivationally twisted heart, prior to any actual sins; (b) this inner sinfulness is the root and source of all actual sins; (c) it derives to us in a real though mysterious way from Adam, our first representative before God. The assertion of original sin makes the point that we are not sinners because we sin, but rather we sin because we are sinners, born with a nature enslaved to sin.

The phrase *total depravity* is commonly used to make explicit the implications of original sin. It signifies a corruption of our moral and spiritual nature that is total not in degree (for no one is as bad as he or she might be) but in extent. It declares that no part of us is untouched by sin, and therefore no action of ours is as good as it should be, and consequently nothing in us or about us ever appears meritorious in God's eyes. We cannot earn God's favor, no matter what we do; unless grace saves us, we are lost.

Total depravity entails total inability, that is, the state of not having it in oneself to respond to God and his Word in a sincere and wholehearted way (John 6:44; Rom. 8:7-8). Paul calls this unresponsiveness of the fallen heart a state of death (Eph. 2:1, 5; Col. 2:13), and the Westminster Confession says: "Man by his fall into a state of sin, hath wholly lost all ability of will to any spiritual good accompanying salvation; so as a natural man, being altogether averse from that good, and dead in sin, is not able by his own strength to convert himself, or to prepare himself thereunto" (IX. 3).

INABILITY

FALLEN HUMAN BEINGS ARE BOTH FREE AND ENSLAVED

The heart is deceitful above all things and beyond cure. Who can understand it?

JEREMIAH 17:9

✝ Clear thought about the fallen human condition requires a distinction between what for the past two centuries has been called free *agency* and what since the start of Christianity has been called free *will*. Augustine, Luther, Calvin, and others spoke of free *will* in two senses, the first trivial, the second important; but this was confusing, and it is better always to use free *agency* for their first sense.

Free agency is a mark of human beings as such. All humans are free agents in the sense that they make their own decisions as to what they will do, choosing as they please in the light of their sense of right and wrong and the inclinations they feel. Thus they are moral agents, answerable to God and each other for their voluntary choices. So was Adam, both before and after he sinned; so are we now, and so are the glorified saints who are confirmed in grace in such a sense that they no longer have it in them to sin. Inability to sin will be one of the delights and glories of heaven, but it will not terminate anyone's humanness; glorified saints will still make choices in accordance with their nature, and those choices will not be any the less the product of human free agency just because they will always be good and right.

Free will, however, has been defined by Christian teachers from the second century on as the ability to choose all the moral options that a situation offers, and Augustine affirmed against Pelagius and most of the Greek Fathers that original sin has robbed us of free will in this sense. We have no natural ability to discern and choose God's way because we have no natural inclination Godward; our hearts are in bondage to sin, and only the grace of regeneration can free us from that slavery. This, for substance, was what Paul taught in Romans 6:16-23; only the *freed* will (Paul says, the freed person) freely and heartily chooses righteousness. A permanent love of righteousness—that is, an inclination of heart to the way of living that pleases God—is one aspect of the freedom that Christ gives (John 8:34-36; Gal. 5:1, 13).

It is worth observing that *will* is an abstraction. My will is not a part of me which I choose to move or not to move, like my hand or my foot; it is precisely me choosing to act and then going into action. The truth about free agency, and about Christ freeing sin's slave from sin's dominion, can be expressed more clearly if the word *will* is dropped and each person says: *I* am the morally responsible free agency; *I* am the slave of sin whom Christ must liberate; *I* am the fallen being who only have it in me to choose against God till God renews my heart.

COVENANT

GOD TAKES SINFUL HUMANS INTO A COVENANT OF GRACE

The LORD had said to Abram, "Leave your country, your people and your father's household and go to the land I will show you. I will make you into a great nation and I will bless you; I will make your name great, and you will be a blessing. I will bless those who bless you, and whoever curses you I will curse; and all peoples on earth will be blessed through you."

GENESIS 12:1-3

✝ Covenants in Scripture are solemn agreements, negotiated or unilaterally imposed, that bind the parties to each other in permanent defined relationships, with specific promises, claims, and obligations on both sides (e.g., the marriage covenant, Mal. 2:14).

When God makes a covenant with his creatures, he alone establishes its terms, as his covenant with Noah and every living creature shows (Gen. 9:9). When Adam and Eve failed to obey the terms of the covenant of works (Gen. 3:6), God did not destroy them, but revealed his covenant of grace to them by promising a Savior (Gen. 3:15). God's covenant rests on his promise, as is clear from his covenant with Abraham. He called Abraham to go to the land that he would give him, and he promised to bless him and to bless all the families of the earth through him (Gen. 12:1-3). Abraham heeded God's call because he believed God's promise; it was his faith in the promise that was credited to him for righteousness (Gen. 15:6; Rom. 4:18-22). God's covenant with Israel at Sinai took the form of a Near Eastern suzerainty treaty, that is, a royal covenant imposed unilaterally on a vassal king and a servant people. Although that covenant required obedience to God's laws under the threat of his curse, it was a continuation of his covenant of grace (Exod. 3:15; Deut. 7:7-8; 9:5-6). God gave his commandments to a people he had already redeemed and claimed (Exod. 19:4; 20:2). The promise of God's covenant was made stronger through the types and shadows of the law given to Moses. The failure of the Israelites to keep the Mosaic covenant showed the need for a new redemption and covenant if God's people were to be truly his and he theirs (Jer. 31:31-34; 32:38-40; cf. Gen. 17:7; Exod. 6:7; 29:45-46; Lev. 11:44-45; 26:12).

God's covenant with Israel was preparation for the coming of God himself, in the person of his Son, to fulfill all his promises and to give substance to the shadows cast by the types (Isa. 40:10; Mal. 3:1; John 1:14; Heb. 7–10). Jesus Christ, the mediator of the new covenant, offered himself as the true and final sacrifice for sin. He obeyed the law perfectly, and as the second representative head of the human race he became the inheritor of all the covenant blessings of pardon, peace, and fellowship with God in his renewed creation, which blessings he now bestows upon believers. The typical and temporary arrangements for imparting those blessings were done away with through the realizing of that which they anticipated. Christ's sending of the Spirit from the throne of his glory seals God's people as his, even as he gives himself to them (Eph. 1:13-14; 2 Cor. 1:22).

As Hebrews 7–10 explains, God brought in an enhanced version of his one eternal covenant with sinners (13:20)—a better covenant with better promises (8:6) based on a better sacrifice (9:23) offered by a better high priest in a better sanctuary (7:26–8:6; 8:11, 13-14), and guaranteeing a better hope than the former version of the covenant ever made explicit, that is, endless glory with God in "a better country—a heavenly one" (11:16; cf. v. 40).

The fulfillment of the old covenant in Christ opens the door of faith to the Gentiles. The "seed of Abraham," the defined community with which the covenant was made, was redefined in Christ. Gentiles with Jews who are united to Christ by faith become Abraham's seed in him (Gal. 3:26-29), while no one outside of Christ can be in covenant with God (Rom. 4:9-17; 11:13-24).

The goal of God's covenantal dealings is, as it always was, the gathering and sanctifying of the covenant people "from every nation, tribe, people and language" (Rev. 7:9), who will one day inhabit new Jerusalem in a renewed world order (21:1-2). Here the covenant relationship will find its fullest expression—"they will be his people, and God himself will be with them and be their God" (21:3). Toward this goal God's shaping of world events still moves.

The covenant framework embraces the entire economy of God's sovereign grace. Christ's heavenly ministry continues to be that of the "mediator of a new covenant" (Heb. 12:24). Salvation is covenant salvation: justification and adoption, regeneration and sanctification are covenant mercies; election was God's choice of future members of his covenant community, the church; baptism and the Lord's Supper, corresponding to circumcision and Passover, are covenant ordinances; God's law is covenant law, and keeping it is the truest expression of gratitude for covenant grace and of loyalty to our covenant God. Covenanting with God in response to his covenanting with us should be a regular devotional exercise for all believers, both in private and at the Lord's Table. An understanding of the covenant of grace guides us through, and helps us to appreciate all the wonders of God's redeeming love.

LAW

GOD LEGISLATES,
AND DEMANDS OBEDIENCE

Moses summoned all Israel and said: Hear,
O Israel, the decrees and laws I declare in
your hearing today. Learn them and be sure
to follow them.

DEUTERONOMY 5:1

✝ Man was not created autonomous, that is, free to be
a law to himself, but theonomous, that is, bound to
keep the law of his Maker. This was no hardship, for God
had so constructed him that grateful obedience would
have brought him highest happiness; duty and delight
would have coincided, as they did in Jesus (John 4:34; cf.
Pss. 112:1; 119:14, 16, 47-48, 97-113, 127-128, 163-167).
The fallen human heart dislikes God's law, both because it
is a law and because it is God's; those who know Christ,
however, find not only that they love the law and want to
keep it, out of gratitude for grace (Rom. 7:18-22; 12:1-2),
but also that the Holy Spirit leads them into a degree of
obedience, starting with the heart, that was never theirs
before (Rom. 7:6; 8:4-6; Heb. 10:16).

God's moral law is abundantly set forth in Scripture, the
Decalogue (the Ten Commandments), other Mosaic statutes, sermons by the prophets, the teaching of Jesus, and
the New Testament letters. It reflects his holy character

and his purposes for created human beings. God commands the behavior that he loves to see and forbids that which offends him. Jesus summarizes the moral law in the two great commandments, love your God and love your neighbor (Matt. 22:37-40), on which, he says, all the Old Testament moral instructions "hang" (depend). The moral teaching of Christ and his apostles is the old law deepened and reapplied to new circumstances—life in the kingdom of God, where the Savior reigns, and in the post-Pentecost era of the Spirit, where God's people are called to live heaven's life among themselves and to be God's counter-culture in the world.

Biblical law is of various sorts. Moral laws command personal and community behavior that is always our duty. The political laws of the Old Testament applied principles of the moral law to Israel's national situation when Israel was a church-state, God's people on earth. The Old Testament laws about ceremonial purity, diet, and sacrifice were temporary enactments for instructional purposes which the New Testament cancels (Matt. 15:20; Mark 7:15-19; 1 Tim. 4:3-5; Heb. 10:1-14, 13:9-10) because their symbolic meaning had been fulfilled. The juxtaposing of moral, judicial, and ritual law in the Mosaic books carried the message that life under God is to be seen and lived not compartmentally but as a many-sided unity, and also that God's authority as legislator gave equal force to the entire code. However, the laws were of different kinds, with different purposes, and the political and ceremonial laws were of limited application, and it seems clear both from the immediate context and from the rest of his teaching that Jesus' affirmation of the unchanging universal force of God's law relates to the moral law as such (Matt. 5:17-19; cf. Luke 16:16-17).

God requires the total obedience of each total person to the total implications of his law as given. It binds "the whole man . . . unto entire obedience for ever"; "it is spiritual, and so reacheth the understanding, will, affections, and all other powers of the soul as well as the words, works, and gestures" (in other words, desiring must be right as well as doings, and Pharisaic externality is not enough: Matt. 15:7-8; 23:25-28); and the corollaries of the law are part of its content—"where a duty is commanded, the contrary sin is forbidden; and, where a sin is forbidden, the contrary duty is commanded" (Westminster Larger Catechism Q.99).

LAW IN ACTION

GOD'S MORAL LAW HAS THREE PURPOSES

I would not have known what sin was except through the law.

ROMANS 7:7

✝ Scripture shows that God intends his law to function in three ways, which Calvin crystallized in classic form for the church's benefit as the law's threefold use.

Its first function is to be a mirror reflecting to us both the perfect righteousness of God and our own sinfulness and shortcomings. Thus "the law bids us, as we try to fulfill its requirements, and become wearied in our weakness under it, to know how to ask the help of grace" (Augustine). The law is meant to give knowledge of sin (Rom. 3:20; 4:15; 5:13; 7:7-11) and, by showing us our need of pardon and our danger of damnation, to lead us in repentance and faith to Christ (Gal. 3:19-24).

Its second function is to restrain evil. Though it cannot change the heart, the law can to some extent inhibit lawlessness by its threats of judgment, especially when backed by a civil code that administers present punishment for proven offenses (Deut. 13:6-11; 19:16-21; Rom. 13:3-4). Thus it secures some civil order and goes some way to protect the righteous from the unjust.

Its third function is to guide the regenerate into the

good works that God has planned for them (Eph. 2:10). The law tells God's children what will please their heavenly Father. It could be called their family code. Christ was speaking of this third use of the law when he said that those who become his disciples must be taught to keep the law and to do all that he had commanded (Matt. 5:18-20, 28:20), and that it is obedience to his commands that will prove the reality of one's love for him (John 14:15). The Christian is free from the law as a supposed system of salvation (Rom. 6:14; 7:4, 6; 1 Cor. 9:20; Gal. 2:15-19; 3:25) but is "under Christ's law" as a rule of life (1 Cor. 9:21; Gal. 6:2).

CONSCIENCE
GOD TEACHES AND
CLEANSES THE HEART

*The earth is defiled by its people; they have
disobeyed the laws, violated the statutes and
broken the everlasting covenant.*

ISAIAH 24:5

✝ Conscience is the built-in power of our minds to
pass moral judgments on ourselves, approving or
disapproving our attitudes, actions, reactions, thoughts,
and plans, and telling us, if it disapproves of what we have
done, that we ought to suffer for it. Conscience has in it
two elements, (a) an awareness of certain things as being
right and wrong, and (b) an ability to apply laws and rules
to specific situations. Conscience, as distinct from our
other powers of mind, is unique; it feels like a person
detached from us, often speaking when we would like it to
be silent and saying things that we would rather not hear.
We can decide whether to heed conscience, but we cannot
decide whether or not it will speak; our experience is that
it decides that for itself. Because of its insistence on judging us by the highest standard we know, we call it God's
voice in the soul, and to that extent so it is.

Paul says that God has written some of the requirements of his law on every human heart (Rom. 2:14-15),
and experience confirms this. ("Heart" in Scripture is

often synonymous with "conscience": the NIV rightly renders the Hebrew "David's heart hit him" as "David was conscience-stricken" in 1 Sam. 24:5, and there are other examples.) But conscience may be misinformed, or conditioned to regard evil as good, or seared and dulled by repeated sin (1 Tim. 4:2), and in such cases conscience will be less than God's voice. The particular judgments of conscience are to be received as God's voice only when they match God's own truth and law in Scripture. Consciences must therefore be educated to judge scripturally.

The consciences of individuals are likely to reflect family and community standards, or lack of them. The book of Judges tells grisly stories of things done at a time when "everyone did as he saw fit" (17:6; 21:25).

Superstition or scruple may lead a person to view as sinful an action that God's Word declares is not sinful; but for such a "weak" conscience (Rom. 14:1-2; 1 Cor. 8:7, 12) to do what it thinks sinful would be sin (Rom. 14:23), and therefore "weak" persons should never be pressed to do what they cannot conscientiously do.

The New Testament ideal is a conscience that is "good" and "clean" (because righteousness is one's purpose, and sin is being avoided: Acts 24:16; 1 Tim. 1:5, 19; Heb. 13:18; 1 Pet. 3:16). But for this our conscience must first be "cleansed" by the blood of Christ; we must see that because Christ in his sacrificial death endured the suffering due to us for all our wrongdoings, they no longer constitute a barrier to our communion with God (Heb. 9:14).

WORSHIP

GOD GIVES A LITURGICAL PATTERN

Come, let us bow down in worship, let us
kneel before the LORD our Maker; for he is
our God and we are the people of his pasture,
the flock under his care. . . .

PSALM 95:6-7

✝ Worship in the Bible is the due response of rational creatures to the self-revelation of their Creator. It is an honoring and glorifying of God by gratefully offering back to him all the good gifts, and all the knowledge of his greatness and graciousness, that he has given. It involves praising him for what he is, thanking him for what he has done, desiring him to get himself more glory by further acts of mercy, judgment, and power, and trusting him with our concern for our own and others' future well-being. Moods of awestruck wonder and grateful celebration are all part of it: David danced with passionate zeal "before the LORD" when he brought up the ark to Jerusalem, and sat in humble amazement "before the LORD" when he was promised a dynasty, and his worship evidently pleased God on both occasions (2 Sam. 6:14-16; 7:18). Learning from God is worship too: attention to his word of instruction honors him; inattention is an insult. Acceptable worship requires "clean hands and a pure heart" (Ps. 24:4) and a willingness to express one's devotion in works of service as well as in words of adoration.

The basis of worship is the covenant relationship whereby God has bound himself to those whom he has saved and claimed. This was true of Old Testament worship as it is now of Christian worship. The spirit of covenant worship, as the Old Testament models it, is a blend of awe and joy at the privilege of drawing near to the mighty Creator with radical self-humbling and honest confession of sin, folly, and need. Since God is holy and we humans are faulty, it must ever be so in this world. As worship will be central in the life of heaven (Rev. 4:8-11, 5:9-14; 7:9-17; 11:15-18; 15:2-4; 19:1-10), so it must be central in the life of the church on earth, and it should already be the main activity, both private and corporate, in each believer's life (Col. 3:17).

In the Mosaic legislation, God gave his covenant people a full pattern for their worship. All the elements of true worship were included in it, though some of them were typical, pointing forward to Christ and ceasing to be valid after he came. In the book of Psalms, hymns and prayers for use in Israel's worship were provided. Christians rightly use these in worship today, making mental adjustments when the reference is to typical features of the Old Testament dispensation of God's covenant—Israel's earthly king, kingdom, enemies, battles, and experiences of prosperity, impoverishment, and divine discipline, plus what was typical in the Jewish worship pattern.

The main features in the liturgical pattern that God gave to Israel were as follows:

(a) The sabbath, each seventh day following six days for labor: a holy day of rest, to be observed as a memorial of

Creation (Gen. 2:3; Exod. 20:8-11) and redemption (Deut. 5:12-15). God insisted on sabbath-keeping (Exod. 16:21-30; 20:8-9; 31:12-17; 34:21; 35:1-3; Lev. 19:3, 30; 23:3; cf. Isa. 58:13-14) and made sabbath-breaking a capital offense (Exod. 31:14; Num. 15:32-36).

(b) Three annual national feasts (Exod. 23:14-17; 34:23; Deut. 16:16) in which the people gathered in God's sanctuary to offer sacrifices celebrating his bounty, to seek and acknowledge reconciliation and fellowship with him, and to eat and drink together as an expression of joy. The feast of Passover and Unleavened Bread, held on the fourteenth day of the first month, commemorated the Exodus (Exod. 12; Lev. 23:5-8; Num. 28:16-25; Deut. 16:1-8); the Feast of Weeks, also called the Feast of Harvest and the Day of Firstfruits, marked the end of the grain harvest, and was held fifty days after the sabbath that began Passover (Exod. 23:16; 34:22; Lev. 23:15-22; Num. 28:26-31; Deut. 16:9-12); and the Feast of Tabernacles or Booths, also called the Feast of Ingathering, held from the fifteenth to the twenty-second day of the seventh month, celebrated the end of the agricultural year, as well as being a reminder of how God led Israel through the desert (Lev. 23:39-43; Num. 29:12-38; Deut. 16:13-15).

(c) The Day of Atonement, held on the tenth day of the seventh month, when the high priest took blood into the central shrine of the sanctuary to atone for Israel's sins during the previous year, and the scapegoat went into the desert as a sign that those sins were now gone (Lev. 16).

(d) The regular sacrificial system, involving daily and monthly burnt offerings (Num. 28:1-15) plus a variety of personal sacrifices, the common features of which were that anything offered must be flawless and that, when an animal was offered, its blood must be poured out on the altar of burnt offering to make atonement (Lev. 17:11).

Rituals of personal purification (Lev. 12–15; Num. 19) and devotion (e.g., consecration of the firstborn, Exod. 13:1-16) were also part of the God-given pattern.

Under the new covenant, in which Old Testament types give way to their antitypes, Christ's priesthood, sacrifice, and intercession supersede the entire Mosaic system for putting away sin (Heb. 7–10); baptism (Matt. 28:19) and the Lord's Supper (Matt. 26:26-29; 1 Cor. 11:23-26) replace circumcision (Gal. 2:3-5; 6:12-16) and Passover (1 Cor. 5:7-8); the Jewish festal calendar no longer binds (Gal. 4:10; Col. 2:16); notions of ceremonial defilement and purification, imposed by God to enforce awareness that some things cut one off from God, cease to apply (Mark 7:19; 1 Tim. 4:3-4); the sabbath is renewed with a casuistry of doing good rather than doing nothing (Luke 13:10-16; 14:1-6), and re-counted, on the basis of one-plus-six rather than six-plus-one. It seems clear that the apostles taught Christians to worship on the first day of the week, the day of Jesus' resurrection, "the Lord's day" (Acts 20:7; Rev. 1:10), treating it as the Christian sabbath. These changes were momentous, but the pattern of praise, thanks, desire, trust, purity, and service, which constitutes true worship, continues unchanged to this day.

PROPHETS

GOD SENT MESSENGERS TO DECLARE HIS WILL

I will raise up for them a prophet like you from among their brothers; I will put my words in his mouth, and he will tell them everything I command him.

DEUTERONOMY 18:18

✝ The canonical prophets, whose books make up over a quarter of the Old Testament, were called by God to be organs and channels of revelation. They were men of God who stood in his council (Jer. 23:22), knew his mind, and were enabled to declare it. God the Holy Spirit spoke in and through them (2 Pet. 1:19-21; Isa. 61:1; Mic. 3:8; Acts 28:25-27; 1 Pet. 1:10-12). They knew he was doing so; hence they dared to start messages with "this is what the LORD says" or "an oracle of the LORD," and to present Yahweh himself as the speaker of what they were saying.

Prophecy involved prediction (foretelling), but usually this was done in a context of declaring God's warnings and exhortations to his covenant people here and now (forthtelling). The predictions had to do with the coming of God's king and kingdom after purging judgments; the prophets' chief concern was to exhort to repentance, in hope that for the present the judgments might be averted.

They were primarily reformers, enforcing God's law and recalling God's people to the covenant faithfulness from which they should never have lapsed.

With their preaching to the nation went prayer for the nation: they talked to God about people just as earnestly as they talked to people about God, and they fulfilled a unique ministry as intercessors (Exod. 32:30-32 [Moses]; 1 Sam. 7:5-9; 12:19-23 [Samuel]; 2 Kings 19:4 [Isaiah]; cf. Jer. 7:16; 11:14; 14:11).

False prophets were a bane to Israel. Professionally linked with Israel's organized worship, they said what people wanted to hear and spoke their own dreams and opinions rather than words of God (1 Kings 22:1-28; Jer. 23:9-40; Ezek. 13).

In the New Testament, one book, Revelation, announces itself as a true and trustworthy prophecy, received directly from God (actually, from God the Father through Jesus Christ: Rev. 1:1-3; 22:12-20). The ministry of the apostles brought instruction directly from God to his people, just as the Old Testament prophetic ministry had done, though the form of presentation was different. Prophets of the New Testament period were linked with the apostles in the foundation of the church (Eph. 2:20; 3:5) as expositors of the fulfillment in Christ of Old Testament hopes (Rom. 16:25-27). The book of Hebrews may well be an example of this kind of prophetic ministry.

INCARNATION

GOD SENT HIS SON, TO SAVE US

*The Word became flesh and made his
dwelling among us. We have seen his glory,
the glory of the One and Only, who came
from the Father, full of grace and truth.*

JOHN 1:14

✝ Trinity and Incarnation belong together. The doctrine of the Trinity declares that the man Jesus is
truly divine; that of the Incarnation declares that the
divine Jesus is truly human. Together they proclaim the
full reality of the Savior whom the New Testament sets
forth, the Son who came from the Father's side at the
Father's will to become the sinner's substitute on the cross
(Matt. 20:28; 26:36-46; John 1:29; 3:13-17; Rom. 5:8;
8:32; 2 Cor. 5:19-21; 8:9; Phil. 2:5-8).

The moment of truth regarding the doctrine of the Trinity came at the Council of Nicaea (A.D. 325), when the
church countered the Arian idea that Jesus was God's first
and noblest creature by affirming that he was of the same
"substance" or "essence" (i.e., the same existing entity) as the
Father. Thus there is one God, not two; the distinction
between Father and Son is within the divine unity, and the
Son is God in the same sense as the Father is. In saying that
Son and Father are "of one substance," and that the Son is
"begotten" (echoing "only-begotten," John 1:14, 18; 3:16,

18, and NIV text notes) but "not made," the Nicene Creed unequivocally recognized the deity of the man from Galilee.

A crucial event for the church's confession of the doctrine of the Incarnation came at the Council of Chalcedon (A.D. 451), when the church countered both the Nestorian idea that Jesus was two personalities—the Son of God and a man—under one skin, and the Eutychian idea that Jesus' divinity had swallowed up his humanity. Rejecting both, the council affirmed that Jesus is one divine-human person in two natures (i.e., with two sets of capacities for experience, expression, reaction, and action); and that the two natures are united in his personal being without mixture, confusion, separation, or division; and that each nature retained its own attributes. In other words, all the qualities and powers that are in us, as well as all the qualities and powers that are in God, were, are, and ever will be really and distinguishably present in the one person of the man from Galilee. Thus the Chalcedonian formula affirms the full humanity of the Lord from heaven in categorical terms.

The Incarnation, this mysterious miracle at the heart of historic Christianity, is central in the New Testament witness. That Jews should ever have come to such a belief is amazing. Eight of the nine New Testament writers, like Jesus' original disciples, were Jews, drilled in the Jewish axiom that there is only one God and that no human is divine. They all teach, however, that Jesus is God's Messiah, the Spirit-annointed son of David promised in the Old Testament (e.g., Isa. 11:1-5; *Christos*, "Christ," is Greek for Messiah). They all present him in a threefold role as teacher, sin-bearer, and ruler—prophet, priest, and king. And in other words, they all insist that Jesus the Messiah should be personally worshiped and trusted—

which is to say that he is God no less than he is man. Observe how the four most masterful New Testament theologians (John, Paul, the writer of Hebrews, and Peter) speak to this.

John's Gospel frames its eyewitness narratives (John 1:14; 19:35; 21:24) with the declarations of its prologue (1:1-18): that Jesus is the eternal divine *Logos* (Word), agent of Creation and source of all life and light (vv. 1-5, 9), who through becoming "flesh" was revealed as Son of God and source of grace and truth, indeed as "God the only begotten" (vv. 14, 18; NIV text notes). The Gospel is punctuated with "I am" statements that have special significance because *I am* (Greek: *ego eimi*) was used to render God's name in the Greek translation of Exodus 3:14; whenever John reports Jesus as saying *ego eimi*, a claim to deity is implicit. Examples of this are John 8:28, 58, and the seven declarations of his grace as (a) the Bread of Life, giving spiritual food (6:35, 48, 51); (b) the Light of the World, banishing darkness (8:12; 9:5); (c) the gate for the sheep, giving access to God (10:7, 9); (d) the Good Shepherd, protecting from peril (10:11, 14); (e) the Resurrection and Life, overcoming our death (11:25); (f) the Way, Truth, and Life, guiding to fellowship with the Father (14:6); (g) the true Vine, nurturing for fruitfulness (15:1, 5). Climactically, Thomas worships Jesus as "my Lord and my God" (20:28). Jesus then pronounces a blessing on all who share Thomas's faith and John urges his readers to join their number (20:29-31).

Paul quotes from what seems to be a hymn that declares Jesus' personal deity (Phil. 2:6); states that "in Christ all the fullness of the Deity lives in bodily form" (Col. 2:9; cf. 1:19); hails Jesus the Son as the Father's image and as his agent in creating and upholding everything (Col. 1:15-

17); declares him to be "Lord" (a title of kingship, with divine overtones), to whom one must pray for salvation according to the injunction to call on Yahweh in Joel 2:32 (Rom. 10:9-13); calls him "God over all" (Rom. 9:5) and "God and Savior" (Titus 2:13); and prays to him personally (2 Cor. 12:8-9), looking to him as a source of divine grace (2 Cor. 13:14). The testimony is explicit: faith in Jesus' deity is basic to Paul's theology and religion.

The writer to the Hebrews, purporting to expound the perfection of Christ's high priesthood, starts by declaring the full deity and consequent unique dignity of the Son of God (Heb. 1:3, 6, 8-12), whose full humanity he then celebrates in chapter 2. The perfection, and indeed the very possibility, of the high priesthood that he describes Christ as fulfilling depends on the conjunction of an endless, unfailing divine life with a full human experience of temptation, pressure, and pain (Heb. 2:14-17; 4:14–5:2; 7:13-28; 12:2-3).

Not less significant is Peter's use of Isaiah 8:12-13 (1 Pet. 3:14). He cites the Greek (Septuagint) version, urging the churches not to fear what others fear but to set apart the Lord as holy. But where the Septuagint text of Isaiah says, "Set apart the Lord himself," Peter writes, "Set apart Christ as Lord" (1 Pet. 3:15). Peter would give the adoring fear due to the Almighty to Jesus of Nazareth, his Master and Lord.

The New Testament forbids worship of angels (Col. 2:18; Rev. 22:8-9) but commands worship of Jesus and focuses consistently on the divine-human Savior and Lord as the proper object of faith, hope, and love here and now. Religion that lacks these emphases is not Christianity. Let there be no mistake about that!

TWO NATURES

JESUS CHRIST IS FULLY HUMAN

Many deceivers, who do not acknowledge
Jesus Christ as coming in the flesh, have
gone out into the world. Any such person is
the deceiver and the antichrist.

2 JOHN 7

✚ Jesus was a man who convinced those closest to him that he was also God; his humanness is not therefore in doubt. John's condemnation of those who denied that "Jesus Christ has come in the flesh" (1 John 4:2-3; 2 John 7) was aimed at Docetists, who replaced the Incarnation with the idea that Jesus was a supernatural visitant (not God) who seemed human but was really a kind of phantom, a teacher who did not really die for sins.

The Gospels show Jesus experiencing human limitations (hunger, Matt. 4:2; weariness, John 4:6; ignorance of fact, Luke 8:45-47) and human pain (weeping at Lazarus' grave, John 11:35, 38; agonizing in Gethsemane, Mark 14:32-42; cf. Luke 12:50; Hebrews 5:7-10; and suffering on the cross). Hebrews stresses that had he not thus experienced human pressures—weakness, temptation, pain— he would not be qualified to help us as we go through these things (Heb. 2:17-18; 4:15-16; 5:2, 7-9). As it is, his human experience is such as to guarantee that in every moment of demand and pressure in our relationship and walk with

God we may go to him, confident that in some sense he has been there before us and so is the helper we need.

Christians, focusing on Jesus' deity, have sometimes thought that it honors Jesus to minimize his humanness. The early heresy of Monophysitism (the idea that Jesus had only one nature) expressed this supposition, as do modern suggestions that he only pretended to be ignorant of facts (on the supposition that he always actualized his omniscience and therefore was aware of everything) and to be hungry and weary (on the supposition that his divinity supernaturally energized his humanity all the time, raising it above the demands of ordinary existence). But Incarnation means, rather, that the Son of God lived his divine-human life in and through his human mind and body at every point, maximizing his identification and empathy with those he had come to save, and drawing on divine resources to transcend human limits of knowledge and energy only when particular requirements of the Father's will so dictated.

The idea that Jesus' two natures were like alternating electrical circuits, so that sometimes he acted in his humanity and sometimes in his divinity, is also mistaken. He did and endured everything, including his sufferings on the cross, in the unity of his divine-human person (i.e., as the Son of God who had taken to himself all human powers of acting, reacting, and experiencing, in their unfallen form). Saying this does not contradict divine impassibility, for impassibility means not that God never experiences distress but that what he experiences, distress included, is experienced at his own will and by his own foreordaining decision.

Jesus, being divine, was impeccable (could not sin), but

this does not mean he could not be tempted. Satan tempted him to disobey the Father by self-gratification, self-display, and self-aggrandizement (Matt. 4:1-11), and the temptation to retreat from the cross was constant (Luke 22:28, where the Greek for "trials" can be translated "temptations"; Matt. 16:23; and Jesus' prayer in Gethsemane). Being human, Jesus could not conquer temptation without a struggle, but being divine it was his nature to do his Father's will (John 5:19, 30), and therefore to resist and fight temptation until he had overcome it. From Gethsemane we may infer that his struggles were sometimes more acute and agonizing than any we ever know. The happy end-result is that "because he himself suffered when he was tempted, he is able to help those who are being tempted" (Heb. 2:18).

VIRGIN BIRTH
JESUS CHRIST WAS BORN
BY MIRACLE

All this took place to fulfill what the Lord
had said through the prophet: "The virgin
will be with child and will give birth to a
son, and they will call him Immanuel"—
which means, "God with us."

MATTHEW 1:22-23

✝ Matthew 1:18-25 and Luke 1:26-56; 2:4-7, two har-
monious and complementary but obviously inde-
pendent stories, unite in witnessing to Jesus' birth as the
consequence of a miraculous conception. Mary became
pregnant by the Holy Spirit's creative action without any
sexual relationship (Matt. 1:20; Luke 1:35).

Most Christians accepted the Virgin Birth without hes-
itation until liberal theology challenged miracles in the
nineteenth century. Then it became a pivotal point in the
debate about Christian supernaturalism and the divinity of
Jesus. Liberalism, seeking to desupernaturalize the faith
and reinterpret Jesus as no more than a uniquely godly and
insightful teacher, surrounded the Virgin Birth with a
spirit of needless and unreasonable skepticism.

In reality, the Virgin Birth meshes harmoniously with
the rest of the New Testament message about Jesus. He
himself worked miracles and rose miraculously from the

111

dead, so no new problem is involved in affirming that he entered the world miraculously. He left the world super-naturally, by resurrection and ascension, so a supernatural way of arriving was entirely fitting. The stress laid on Jesus' preincarnate dignity and glory (John 1:1-9; 17:5; 2 Cor. 8:9; Phil. 2:5-11; Col. 1:15-17; Heb. 1:1-3; 1 John 1:1) made a mode of entry into incarnate life that involved proclamation of the glorious role he was coming to fulfill (Matt. 1:21-23; Luke 1:31-35) more natural than any alter-native.

It is noteworthy that Matthew and Luke show them-selves much more interested in the fulfillment of God's redemptive purpose than in the virginal conception as a physical wonder or an apologetic weapon or a pointer to two-nature christology.

While we cannot affirm that a divine person could not have entered this world any other way than by virgin birth, Jesus' miraculous birth does in fact point to his deity and also to the reality of the creative power that operates in our new birth (John 1:13). Also, while we cannot affirm that God could not have produced sinless humanity apart from virgin birth, Jesus' humanity was sinless, and the circum-stances of his birth call attention to the miracle that was involved when Mary, a sinner (Luke 1:47), gave birth to one who was not "in Adam" as she was, nor therefore needed a Savior as she did. Rather, Jesus was destined through the maintained sinlessness of his unflawed human nature to become the perfect sacrifice for human sins, and so the Savior of his mother and of the rest of the church with her.

TEACHER

JESUS CHRIST PROCLAIMED
GOD'S KINGDOM AND FAMILY

When Jesus had finished saying these things,
the crowds were amazed at his teaching,
because he taught as one who had authority,
and not as their teachers of the law.

MATTHEW 7:28-29

✝ Jesus was Son of God incarnate, and his teaching,
given him by his Father (John 7:16-18; 12:49-50),
will stand forever (Mark 13:31) and finally judge its hear-
ers (John 12:48; Matt. 7:24-27). The importance of paying
attention to it cannot, therefore, be overstressed. Jesus
taught as Jewish rabbis generally did, by bits and pieces
rather than in flowing discourses, and many of his most
vital utterances are in parables, proverbs, and isolated
pronouncements responding to questions and reacting to
situations.

All his public teaching was marked by an authority that
brought amazement (Matt. 7:28-29; Mark 1:27; John
7:46), but some of the teaching was enigmatically expressed, requiring thought and spiritual insight ("ears,"
Matt. 11:15; 13:9, 43; Luke 14:35) and baffling the com-
placent and casual. Jesus' reason for only dropping dark
hints about (for instance) his messianic role, atonement,
resurrection, and forthcoming reign, was twofold: first,

113

only events could make these things clear in any case; and second, Jesus' concern was to call people into discipleship through his personal impact on them, and then teach them about himself within that relationship, rather than to offer detailed theological instruction to the uncommitted. Nonetheless, Jesus' statements often are clear, and many of the fuller presentations in the epistles are best read as so many footnotes to what Jesus said.

Jesus' teaching had three regular points of reference. The first was to his divine Father, who had sent and was now directing him (Matt. 11:25-27; 16:13-17, 27; 21:37; 26:29, 53; Luke 2:49; 22:29; John 3:35; 5:18-23, 26-27, 36-37; 8:26-29; 10:25-30, 36-38), and to whom his disciples must learn to relate as their Father in heaven (Matt. 5:43–6:14, 25-33; 7:11). The second was to people, both individuals and crowds in their lostness (Matt. 9:36; Mark 10:21), the addressees of his constant and many-faceted calls to repentance and a new life (Matt. 4:17; 11:20-24; Mark 1:15; Luke 5:32; 13:3-5; 15:7; 24:47). The third was to himself, as Son of Man, a messianic title (Matt. 16:13-16). "One like a son of man" takes the kingdom in Daniel 7:13-14. For Jesus' own use of this title, see Mark 8:38; 13:26; 14:62 (echoing Daniel); Matthew 12:40; Mark 8:31; 9:31; 10:33, 45; 14:21, 41; Luke 18:31-33 (predicting his death and resurrection); John 3:13-15; 6:27 (declaring his saving ministry).

Out of Jesus' witness to his Father, to people's need, and to his own role, three theological themes take form:

1. *The kingdom of God.* This is a relational reality that came with Jesus as the fulfillment of God's plan for history, of which Old Testament prophets had constantly spoken (Isa. 2:1-4; 9:6-7; 11:1–12:6; 42:1-9; 49:1-7; Jer. 23:5-6).

The kingdom is present with Jesus; his miracles are signs of it (Matt. 11:12; 12:28; Luke 16:16; 17:20-21). The kingdom becomes real and crucial in a person's life when he or she submits in faith to the lordship of Christ, a momentous commitment that brings salvation and eternal life (Mark 10:17-27; John 5:24). The kingdom will be preached and will grow (Matt. 24:14; 13:31-33) until the Son of Man, now reigning in heaven, reappears for judgment and, in the case of his faithful servants, for joy (Matt. 13:24-43, 47-50).

2. *The saving work of Jesus.* Having come down from heaven at the Father's will to bring chosen sinners to glory, Jesus died for them, calls and draws them to himself, forgives their sins, and keeps them safe till the day of their resurrection, glorification, and introduction into heaven's happiness (Luke 5:20, 23; 7:48; John 6:37-40, 44-45; 10:14-18, 27-29; 12:32; 17:1-26).

3. *The ethics of God's family.* The new life, which comes to sinners as a gift of God's free grace, must be expressed in a new life-style. Those who live by grace must practice gratitude; those who have been greatly loved must show great love to others; those who live by being forgiven must themselves forgive; those who know God as their loving heavenly Father must accept his providences without bitterness, honoring him at all times by trusting in his protecting care. In a word, God's children must be like their Father and their Savior, which means being utterly unlike the world (Matt. 5:43-48; 6:12-15; 18:21-35; 20:26-28; 22:35-40).

SINLESSNESS

JESUS CHRIST WAS ENTIRELY
FREE FROM SIN

*He committed no sin, and no deceit was
found in his mouth.*

1 PETER 2:22

✚ The New Testament insists that Jesus was entirely free from sin (John 8:46; 2 Cor. 5:21; Heb. 4:15; 7:26; 1 Pet. 2:22; 1 John 3:5). This means not only that he never disobeyed his Father but that he loved God's law and found wholehearted joy in keeping it. In fallen human beings, there is always some reluctance to obey God, and sometimes resentment amounting to hatred at the claims he makes on us (Rom. 8:7). But Jesus' moral nature was unfallen, as was Adam's prior to his sin, and in Jesus there was no prior inclination away from God for Satan to play on, as there is in us. Jesus loved his Father and his Father's will with all his heart, mind, soul, and strength.

Hebrews 4:15 says that Jesus was "tempted in every way, just as we are," though without sinning. This means that every type of temptation that we face—temptations to wrongfully indulge natural desires of body and mind, to evade moral and spiritual issues, to cut moral corners and take easy ways out, to be less than fully loving and sympathetic and creatively kind to others, to become self-protective and self-pitying, and so on—came upon him, but he yielded to none of them. Overwhelming opposition did not overwhelm him, and through the agony of Gethsemane and the cross he fought temptation and resisted sin to the point where his blood was shed. Christians must learn from him to do likewise (Heb. 12:3-13; Luke 14:25-33).

Jesus' sinlessness was necessary for our salvation. Had he not been "a lamb without blemish or defect" his blood would not have been "precious" (1 Pet. 1:19). He would have needed a savior himself, and his death would not have redeemed us. His active obedience (perfect lifelong conformity to God's law for mankind, and to his revealed will for the Messiah) qualified Jesus to become our Savior by dying for us on the cross. Jesus' passive obedience (enduring the penalty of God's broken law as our sinless substitute) crowned his active obedience to secure the pardon and acceptance of those who put their faith in him (Rom. 5:18-19; 2 Cor. 5:18-21; Phil. 2:8; Heb. 10:5-10).

OBEDIENCE

JESUS CHRIST FULFILLED HIS
FATHER'S REDEMPTIVE WILL

Jesus gave them this answer: "I tell you the
truth, the Son can do nothing by himself;
he can do only what he sees his Father doing,
because whatever the Father does
the Son also does."

JOHN 5:19

✝ Humility in Scripture means, not pretending to be worthless and refusing positions of responsibility, but knowing and keeping the place God has appointed for one. Being humble is a matter of holding on to God's arrangement, whether it means the high exposure of leadership (Moses was humble as a leader, Num. 12:3) or the obscurity of subservience. When Jesus stated matter-of-factly that he was "humble in heart" (Matt. 11:29), he meant that he was conscientiously following the Father's plan for his earthly life.

In this he was keeping his place as the second Person of the Godhead. The three Persons of the Holy Trinity are eternal and self-existent, partaking equally of all aspects and attributes of deity, and always acting together in cooperative solidarity. But the unchanging cooperative pattern is that the second and third Persons identify with the purpose of the first, so that the Son becomes the Father's executive and the Spirit acts as the agent of both. It is the Son's nature and joy to do his Father's will (John 4:34).

Regarding redemption, the Father's will for the Son is sometimes called the covenant of redemption, since it has the form of an agreement between two parties on a program and a promise. The Westminster Confession summarizes the agreement (the Father's purpose, accepted by the Son) as follows:

It pleased God in his eternal purpose, to choose and ordain the Lord Jesus, his only-begotten Son, to be the Mediator between God and man, the Prophet, Priest, and King, the Head and Savior of his Church, the heir of all things, and Judge of the world: unto whom he did from all eternity give a people, to be his seed, and to be by him in time redeemed, called, justified, sanctified, and glorified. (VIII.1)

(For the ideas and phraseology of this statement, see Eph. 3:11; 1 Pet. 1:20; 1 Tim. 2:5; Acts 3:22; Heb. 5:5-6; Luke 1:33; Eph. 5:23; Heb. 1:2; Acts 17:31; Isa. 53:10; John 17:6; 1 Cor. 1:30; Rom. 8:29-30.)

This purpose of the Father for the Son had two stages. The first stage was humiliation. The eternal Son let go of his glory and through incarnation became a poor man and a religious outsider. Finally, by means of a show trial and unscrupulous manipulation of Pilate's moral weakness, he became a condemned criminal dying a dreadful death as mankind's sin-bearer (Phil. 2:6-8; 2 Cor. 8:9; Gal. 3:13; 4:4-5).

The second stage was exaltation. Christ rose, ascended, and now by his Father's appointment reigns as king over the world and the church (Phil. 2:9-11), sending the Holy Spirit (John 15:26; 16:7; Acts 2:33) and thereby applying to us the redemption that by dying he won for us. Drawing those given him to himself (John 12:32), interceding for them (Rom. 8:34; Heb. 7:25; John 17), guarding, guiding, and caring for them as a shepherd cares for his sheep (John 10:27-30), he is currently bringing many sons to glory (Heb. 2:10) according to the Father's plan, and he will continue to do so until all God's elect have come to repentance and new life (2 Pet. 3:9).

In all of this the Son is obeying the Father in true humility, living out a natural, voluntary, and joyful subordination. Meanwhile, the Father's aim of having the Son worshiped and glorified equally with himself is steadily being fulfilled (John 5:19-23).

VOCATION

JESUS CHRIST'S MISSION WAS REVEALED AT HIS BAPTISM

At that time Jesus came from Nazareth in Galilee and was baptized by John in the Jordan. As Jesus was coming up out of the water, he saw heaven being torn open and the Spirit descending on him like a dove. And a voice came from heaven: "You are my Son, whom I love; with you I am well pleased."

MARK 1:9-11

✝ There is continuity between John's baptism of repentance (Mark 1:4) and the trinitarian baptism instituted by Jesus (Matt. 28:19). Both were symbols of cleansing and had remission of sins in view (Mark 1:4; Acts 2:38). They were not identical, however, and those baptized by John needed Christian baptism too (Acts 19:5). Christian baptism is an initiatory sign pointing to a relationship with the Christ who has come (it is called baptism in Christ's name in Acts 2:38; 10:48; 19:5); John's baptism was a preparatory rite, signifying readiness for the coming of the Christ and for his judgment (Matt. 3:7-12; Luke 3:7-18; Acts 19:4).

John's baptism was a radical innovation. Previously, only Gentiles converting to Judaism had been required to undergo a symbolic washing. Now, however, God through

121

John was commanding all Jews to signify their repentance by being publicly washed. Most Jewish leaders thought John's requirement was heretical and insulting (Matt. 21:25-26).

Jesus insisted that John, his cousin, must baptize him, overriding John's protests (Matt. 3:13-15). In his role as Messiah, "born under law" (Gal. 4:4), Jesus had to submit to all God's requirements of Israel and to identify with those whose sins he had come to bear. His baptism proclaimed that he had come to take the sinner's place under God's penal judgment. This is the sense in which he was baptized "to fulfill all righteousness" (Matt. 3:15; cf. Isa. 53:11).

His baptism was a manifestation of the Trinity: the Father spoke from the sky, and the dove descended, a sign of the Spirit's anointing. The meaning of the dove descending and abiding was not that Jesus had not previously been Spirit-filled but that he was now being marked out as the Spirit-bearer who would become the Spirit-baptizer (John 1:32-33) and so bring in the age of the Spirit that was to fulfill Israel's hopes (Luke 4:1, 14, 18-21).

TRANSFIGURATION

HOW JESUS CHRIST'S GLORY
WAS REVEALED

After six days Jesus took Peter, James and
John with him and led them up a high
mountain, where they were all alone. There
he was transfigured before them. His clothes
became dazzling white, whiter than anyone
in the world could bleach them. And there
appeared before them Elijah and Moses,
who were talking with Jesus.

MARK 9:2-4

✝ Recorded in three of the Gospels (Matt. 17:1-8;
Mark 9:2-8; Luke 9:28-36), and evidently planned
by Jesus for Peter, James, and John to see and, later, to
testify to (Matt. 17:9; cf. 2 Pet. 1:16-18; John 1:14), the
Transfiguration was a significant event in the revelation of
Jesus' deity. The transformation that the divine-human
Lord underwent as he prayed (Luke 9:29) was from one
standpoint a taste of things to come: it was a momentary
transition from the concealing of his divine glory that
marked his days on earth to the revealing of that glory
when he returns and we see him as he is. It was a transition
too from humanity as it is in us now to what it will be on
Resurrection Day (Phil. 3:20-21).

The bright light that shone from Jesus through his
clothes as his face changed (Luke 9:29) was the glory

intrinsic to him as the divine Son, "the radiance of God's glory" (Heb. 1:3). The voice from the cloud confirmed the identification that the vision had already given.

The Transfiguration was also a significant event in the revelation of God's kingdom (i.e., the kingdom of the Messiah, God's prophesied Savior-King, in terms of whom God's kingdom is defined). Moses and Elijah represented the law and the prophets' witnessing to Jesus and being superseded by him. The "departure" (Greek: *exodos*) of which they and Jesus talked (Luke 9:31) must have been his death, resurrection, and ascension. This was not just a way of leaving this world but also a way of redeeming his people, just as the *exodos* from Egypt that Moses led was to redeem Israel from bondage.

Following the Transfiguration, Jesus veiled his glory and went down from the mount to minister once more, and in due course to suffer for our salvation. Comments F. B. Meyer: "The door through which Moses and Elijah had come stood open, and by it our Lord might have returned. But he could never, under those circumstance, have been the Saviour of mankind. He knew this, so he set his face toward Calvary."

RESURRECTION

JESUS CHRIST WAS RAISED
FROM THE DEAD

*On the first day of the week, very early in
the morning, the women took the spices they
had prepared and went to the tomb. They
found the stone rolled away from the tomb,
but when they entered, they did not find
the body of the Lord Jesus.*

LUKE 24:1-3

✝ Jesus' resurrection, which was a divine act involving
all three Persons of the Godhead (John 10:17-18;
Acts 13:30-35; Rom. 1:4), was not just a resuscitation of
the ruined physical frame that was taken down from the
cross for burial. It was, rather, a transformation of Jesus'
humanity that enabled him to appear, vanish, and move
unseen from one location to another (Luke 24:31, 36). It
was the creative renewing of his original body, the body
that is now fully glorified and deathless (Phil. 3:21; Heb.
7:16, 24). The Son of God in heaven still lives in and
through that body, and will do so forever. In 1 Corinthians
15:50-54, Paul envisages that Christians who are alive on
earth at the moment of Christ's return will undergo a
similar transformation, though in 2 Corinthians 5:1-5 he
shows himself aware that Christians who die before the
Second Coming will be "clothed" with their new body

(the "eternal house in heaven") as a distinct event, at or after the time of the old body's return to dust (Gen. 3:19).

Christianity rests on the certainty of Jesus' resurrection as a space-time occurrence in history. All four Gospels highlight it, focusing on the empty tomb and resurrection appearances, and Acts insists on it (Acts 1:3; 2:24-35; 3:15; 4:10; 5:30-32; 13:33-37). Paul regarded the Resurrection as indisputable proof that the message about Jesus as Judge and Savior is true (Acts 17:31; 1 Cor. 15:1-11, 20).

Jesus' resurrection demonstrated his victory over death (Acts 2:24; 1 Cor. 15:54-57), vindicated him as righteous (John 16:10), and indicated his divine identity (Rom. 1:4). It led on to his ascension and enthronement (Acts 1:9-11; 2:34; Phil. 2:9-11; cf. Isa. 53:10-12) and his present heavenly reign. It guarantees the believer's present forgiveness and justification (Rom. 4:25; 1 Cor. 15:17) and is the basis of resurrection life in Christ for the believer here and now (John 11:25-26; Rom. 6; Eph. 1:18–2:10; Col. 2:9-15; 3:1-4).

ASCENSION

JESUS CHRIST WAS TAKEN UP INTO HEAVEN

While he was blessing them, he left them and was taken up into heaven.

LUKE 24:51

✝ Jesus' ascension was his Father's act of withdrawing him from his disciples' gaze upward (a sign of exaltation) into a cloud (a sign of God's presence). This was not a form of space travel, but part two (the Resurrection being part one) of Jesus' return from the depths of death to the height of glory. Jesus foretold the Ascension (John 6:62; 14:2, 12; 16:5, 10, 17, 28; 17:5; 20:17), and Luke described it (Luke 24:50-53; Acts 1:6-11). Paul celebrated it and affirmed Christ's consequent lordship (Eph. 1:20; 4:8-10; Phil. 2:9-11; 1 Tim. 3:16), and the writer of Hebrews applied this truth for encouragement of the fainthearted (Heb. 1:3; 4:14; 9:24). The fact that Jesus Christ is enthroned as master of the universe should be of enormous encouragement to all believers.

The Ascension was from one standpoint the restoration of the glory that the Son had before the Incarnation, from another the glorifying of human nature in a way that had never happened before, and from a third the start of a reign that had not previously been exercised in this form. The Ascension establishes three facts:

1. *Christ's personal ascendancy.* Jesus went up to the place of power, pictured as a throne at the Father's right hand. To sit on such a throne, as the Grand Vizier in the Persian court used to do, is to occupy the position of executive ruler on the monarch's behalf (Matt. 28:18; Eph. 1:20-22; 1 Cor. 15:27; 1 Pet. 3:22).

2. *Christ's spiritual omnipresence.* In the heavenly sanctuary in heavenly Zion (Heb. 9:24; 12:22-24), Jesus is accessible to all who invoke him (Heb. 4:14), and he is powerful to help them, anywhere in the world (Heb. 4:16; 7:25; 13:6-8).

3. *Christ's heavenly ministry.* The reigning Lord intercedes for his people (Rom. 8:34; Heb. 7:25). Though requesting from the Father is part of the interceding activity (John 14:16), the essence of Christ's intercession is intervention in our interest (from his throne) rather than supplication on our behalf (as if his position were one of sympathy without status or authority). In sovereignty he now lavishes upon us the benefits that his suffering won for us. "He pleads [for us]—by his presence on his Father's throne" (B. F. Westcott). "Our Lord's life in heaven is his prayer" (H. B. Swete). From his throne he sends the Holy Spirit constantly to enrich his people (Acts 2:33; John 16:7-14) and equip them for service (Eph. 4:8-12).

SESSION
JESUS REIGNS IN HEAVEN

After he had provided purification for sins,
he sat down at the right hand
of the Majesty in heaven.

HEBREWS 1:3

Christ's present role in glory is commonly referred to as his "heavenly session." *Session* (Latin: *sessio*) means "sitting." The New Testament can picture Jesus' heavenly activity as standing ready to act (Acts 7:56; Rev. 1:1–16; 14:1), walking among his people (Rev. 2:1), and riding to battle (Rev. 19:11-16), but it regularly expresses his present authority by saying that he sits at the Father's right hand—not to rest, but to rule. The picture is not of inactivity but of authority.

In Psalm 110 God sets the Messiah at his right hand as king and priest—as king to see all his enemies under his feet (v. 1), and as priest to serve God and channel God's grace forever (v. 4). Though personally the Messiah may be out fighting (vv. 2-3, 5-7), positionally he is always sitting at Yahweh's right hand. In Acts 2:34-35, Hebrews 1:13 and 10:12, and Matthew 22:44, this picture is applied directly to Jesus Christ, who since the Ascension actively reigns in the mediatorial kingdom of God.

Christ rules over all the spheres of authority that exist, both angelic and human (Matt. 28:18; 1 Pet. 3:22). His kingdom in a direct sense is the church, which he heads as his body and governs by his Word and Spirit (Eph. 1:22-23). The state is not the form of the kingdom of God as it was in the Old Testament: the sword is not to be used to enforce Christ's kingdom (John 18:36), but Christ from his throne uses secular authority to maintain civil peace and order, and he commands his disciples to submit to its rules (Matt. 22:21; Rom. 13:1-7). Christians take great comfort in knowing that Christ is Lord of all; they seek in every sphere of life to do his will and to remind themselves and others that all are accountable to Christ as Judge, whether they be governors or governed, husbands or wives, parents or children, employers or employees. All rational beings will finally give account of themselves to Christ as Judge (Matt. 25:31; Acts 17:31; Rom. 2:16; 2 Cor. 5:10).

Christ's session will continue until all his and our enemies, including death, are brought to nothing. Death, the last enemy, will cease to be when Christ at his appearing raises the dead for judgment (John 5:28-29). Once judgment has been executed, the work of the mediatorial kingdom will be over, and Christ will triumphantly deliver the kingdom to the Father (1 Cor. 15:24-28).

MEDIATION

JESUS CHRIST IS THE MEDIATOR BETWEEN GOD AND MAN

*For there is one God and one mediator
between God and men, the man Christ Jesus.*

1 TIMOTHY 2:5

✝ The saving ministry of Jesus Christ is summed up in the statement that he is the "mediator between God and men" (1 Tim. 2:5). A mediator is a go-between who brings together parties who are not in communication and who may be alienated, estranged, and at war with each other. The mediator must have links with both sides in order to identify with and maintain the interests of both and represent each to the other on a basis of good will. Thus Moses was mediator between God and Israel (Gal. 3:19), speaking to Israel on God's behalf when God gave the law (Exod. 20:18-21) and speaking to God on Israel's behalf when Israel had sinned (Exod. 32:9–33:17).

Every member of our fallen and rebellious race is by nature "hostile to God" (Rom. 8:7) and stands under God's wrath (i.e., the punitive rejection whereby as Judge he expresses active anger at our sins, Rom. 1:18; 2:5-9; 3:5-6). Reconciliation of the warring parties is needed, but this can occur only if God's wrath is somehow absorbed and quenched and man's anti-God heart, which motivates his anti-God life, is somehow changed. In mercy, God the angry Judge sent his Son into the world to bring about the needed reconciliation. It was not that the kindly Son acted to placate his harsh Father; the initiative was the Father's own. In Calvin's words, "in an inconceivable way he loved us even when he hated us," and his gift to us of the Son as our sin bearer was the fruit of that love (John 3:14-16; Rom. 5:5-8; 1 John 4:8-10). In all his mediatorial ministry the Son was doing his Father's will.

Objectively and once for all, Christ achieved reconciliation for us through penal substitution. On the cross he took our place, carried our identity as it were, bore the curse due to us (Gal. 3:13), and by his sacrificial blood-shedding made peace for us (Eph. 2:16; Col. 1:20). *Peace* here means an end to hostility, guilt, and exposure to the retributive punishment that was otherwise unavoidable—in other words, pardon for all the past and permanent personal acceptance for the future. Those who have received reconciliation through faith in Christ are justified and have peace with God (Rom. 5:1, 10). The mediator's present work, which he carries forward through human messengers, is to persuade those for whom he achieved reconciliation actually to receive it (John 12:32; Rom. 15:18; 2 Cor. 5:18-21; Eph. 2:17).

Jesus is "the mediator of a new covenant" (Heb. 9:15; 12:24)—that is, the initiator of a new relationship of conscious peace with God, going beyond what the less effective Old Testament arrangements for dealing with the guilt of sin could ever secure (Heb. 9:11–10:18).

One of Calvin's great contributions to Christian understanding was his observation that the New Testament writers expound Jesus' mediatorial ministry in terms of the threefold office ("office" means set task, or defined role) of prophet, priest, and king.

The three aspects of Christ's work are found together in the letter to the Hebrews, where Jesus is both the messianic king, exalted to his throne (1:3, 13; 4:16; 2:9), and also the great High Priest (2:17; 4:14–5:10; chs. 7–10), who offered himself to God as a sacrifice for our sins. In addition, Christ is the messenger ("apostle," the one sent to announce, 3:1) through whom the message of which he is himself the substance was first spoken (2:3). In Acts 3:22 Jesus is called a prophet for the same reason that Hebrews calls him an apostle, namely, because he instructed people by declaring to them the Word of God.

While in the Old Testament the mediating roles of prophet, priest, and king were fulfilled by separate individuals, all three offices now coalesce in the one person of Jesus. It is his glory, given him by the Father, to be in this way the all-sufficient Savior. We who believe are called to understand this and to show ourselves his people by obeying him as our king, trusting him as our priest, and learning from him as our prophet and teacher. To center on Jesus Christ in this way is the hallmark of authentic Christianity.

SACRIFICE
JESUS CHRIST MADE ATONEMENT FOR SIN

God presented him as a sacrifice of atonement, through faith in his blood. . . .

ROMANS 3:25

✝ *Atonement* means making amends, blotting out the offense, and giving satisfaction for wrong done; thus reconciling to oneself the alienated other and restoring the disrupted relationship.

Scripture depicts all human beings as needing to atone for their sins but lacking all power and resources for doing so. We have offended our holy Creator, whose nature it is to hate sin (Jer. 44:4; Hab. 1:13) and to punish it (Ps. 5:4-6; Rom. 1:18; 2:5-9). No acceptance by, or fellowship with, such a God can be expected unless atonement is made, and since there is sin in even our best actions, anything we do in hopes of making amends can only increase our guilt or worsen our situation. This makes it ruinous folly to seek to establish one's own righteousness before God (Job 15:14-16; Rom. 10:2-3); it simply cannot be done.

But against this background of human hopelessness, Scripture sets forth the love, grace, mercy, pity, kindness, and compassion of God, the offended Creator, in himself providing the atonement that our sin has made necessary. This amazing grace is the focal center of New Testament faith, hope, worship, ethics, and spiritual life; from Matthew to Revelation it shines out with breathtaking glory.

When God brought Israel out of Egypt, he set up as part of the covenant relationship a system of sacrifices that had at its heart the shedding and offering of the blood of unflawed animals "to make atonement for yourselves" (Lev. 17:11). These sacrifices were *typical* (that is, as *types*, they pointed forward to something else). Though sins were in fact "left . . . unpunished" (Rom. 3:25) when sacrifices were faithfully offered, what actually blotted them out was not the animals' blood (Heb. 10:11) but the blood of the *antitype*, the sinless Son of God, Jesus Christ, whose death on the cross atoned for all sins that were remitted before the event as well as sins committed after it (Rom. 3:25-26; 4:3-8; Heb. 9:11-15).

New Testament references to the blood of Christ are regularly sacrificial (e.g., Rom. 3:25; 5:9; Eph. 1:7; Rev. 1:5). As a perfect sacrifice for sin (Rom. 8:3; Eph. 5:2; 1 Pet. 1:18-19), Christ's death was our redemption (i.e., our rescue by ransom: the paying of a price that freed us from the jeopardy of guilt, enslavement to sin, and expectation of wrath; Rom. 3:24; Gal. 4:4-5; Col. 1:14). Christ's death was God's act of reconciling us to himself, overcoming his own hostility to us that our sins provoked (Rom. 5:10; 2 Cor. 5:18-19; Col. 1:20-22). The Cross propitiated God (i.e., quenched his wrath against us by expiating our sins and so removing them from his sight). Key texts here are Romans 3:25; Hebrews 2:17; 1 John 2:2 and 4:10, in each of which the Greek expresses propitiation explicitly. The cross had this propitiatory effect because in his suffering Christ assumed our identity, as it were, and endured the retributive judgment due to us ("the curse of the law,"

Gal. 3:13) as our substitute, in our place, with the damning record of our transgressions nailed by God to his cross as the tally of crimes for which he was now dying (Col. 2:14; cf. Matt. 27:37; Isa. 53:4-6; Luke 22:37).

Christ's atoning death ratified the inauguration of the new covenant, in which access to God under all circumstances is guaranteed by Christ's one sacrifice that covers all transgressions (Matt. 26:27-28; 1 Cor. 11:25; Heb. 9:15; 10:12-18). Those who through faith in Christ have "received reconciliation" (Rom. 5:11) "in him . . . become the righteousness of God" (2 Cor. 5:21). In other words, they are justified and receive the status of adopted children in God's family (Gal. 4:5). Thereafter they live under the motivating constraint and control of the love of Christ for them as made known and measured by the cross (2 Cor. 5:14).

DEFINITE REDEMPTION
JESUS CHRIST DIED
FOR GOD'S ELECT

*I am the good shepherd; I know my sheep
and my sheep know me—just as the Father
knows me and I know the Father—and I lay
down my life for the sheep.*

JOHN 10:14, 15

Definite redemption, sometimes called "particular redemption," "effective atonement," and "limited atonement," is an historic Reformed doctrine about the intention of the triune God in the death of Jesus Christ. Without doubting the infinite worth of Christ's sacrifice or the genuineness of God's "whoever will" invitation to all who hear the gospel (Rev. 22:17), the doctrine states that the death of Christ actually put away the sins of all God's elect and ensured that they would be brought to faith through regeneration and kept in faith for glory, and that this is what it was intended to achieve. From this definiteness and effectiveness follows its limitedness: Christ did not die in this efficacious sense for everyone. The proof of that, as Scripture and experience unite to teach us, is that not all are saved.

The only possible alternatives are (a) actual universalism, holding that Christ's death guaranteed salvation for every member of the human race, past, present, and future, or (b) hypothetical universalism, holding that Christ's death made salvation possible for everyone but actual only for those who add to it a response of faith and repentance that was not secured by it. The choices are, therefore, an atonement of unlimited efficacy but limited extent (Reformed particularism), one of unlimited extent but limited efficacy (hypothetical universalism), or one of unlimited efficacy and unlimited extent (actual universalism). Scripture must be the guide in choosing between these possibilities.

Scripture speaks of God as having chosen for salvation a great number of our fallen race and having sent Christ into the world to save them (John 6:37-40; 10:27-29; 11:51-52; Rom. 8:28-39; Eph. 1:3-14; 1 Pet. 1:20). Christ is regularly said to have died for particular groups or persons, with the clear implication that his death secured their salvation (John 10:15-18, 27-29; Rom. 5:8-10; 8:32; Gal. 2:20, 3:13-14; 4:4-5; 1 John 4:9-10; Rev. 1:4-6; 5:9-10). Facing his passion, he prayed only for those the Father had given him, not for the "world" (i.e., the rest of mankind, John 17:9, 20). Is it conceivable that he would decline to pray for any whom he intended to die for? Definite redemption is the only one of the three views that harmonizes with this data.

There is no inconsistency or incoherence in the teaching of the New Testament about, on the one hand, the offer of Christ in the gospel, which Christians are told to make known everywhere, and, on the other hand, the fact that Christ achieved a totally efficacious redemption for God's elect on the cross. It is a certain truth that all who come to Christ in faith will find mercy (John 6:35, 47-51,

54-57; Rom. 1:16; 10:8-13). The elect hear Christ's offer, and through hearing it are effectually called by the Holy Spirit. Both the invitation and the effectual calling flow from Christ's sin-bearing death. Those who reject the offer of Christ do so of their own free will (i.e., because they choose to, Matt. 22:1-7; John 3:18), so that their final perishing is their own fault. Those who receive Christ learn to thank him for the cross as the centerpiece of God's plan of sovereign saving grace.

PART TI·REE

GOD REVEALED AS LORD OF GRACE

PARACLETE

THE HOLY SPIRIT MINISTERS
TO BELIEVERS

*When he, the Spirit of truth, comes, he will
guide you into all truth. He will not speak
on his own; he will speak only what he hears,
and he will tell you what is yet to come. He
will bring glory to me by taking from what
is mine and making it known to you.*

JOHN 16:13-14

✝ Before Jesus' passion, he promised that the Father
and he would send his disciples "another Counselor" (John 14:16, 26; 15:26; 16:7). The Counselor or
Paraclete, from the Greek word *parakletos* (meaning one
who gives support), is a helper, adviser, strengthener, en-
courager, ally, and advocate. *Another* points to the fact that
Jesus was the first Paraclete and is promising a replacement who, after he is gone, will carry on the teaching and
testimony that he started (John 16:6-7).

Paraclete ministry, by its very nature, is personal, relational ministry, implying the full personhood of the one
who fulfills it. Though the Old Testament said much
about the Spirit's activity in Creation (e.g., Gen. 1:2; Ps.
33:6), revelation (e.g., Isa. 61:1-6; Mic. 3:8), enabling for
service (e.g., Exod. 31:2-6; Judg. 6:34; 15:14-15; Isa. 11:2),
and inward renewal (e.g., Ps. 51:10-12; Ezek. 36:25-27), it

143

did not make clear that the Spirit is a distinct divine Person. In the New Testament, however, it becomes clear that the Spirit is as truly a Person distinct from the Father as the Son is. This is apparent not only from Jesus' promise of "another Counselor," but also from the fact that the Spirit, among other things, speaks (Acts 1:16; 8:29; 10:19; 11:12; 13:2; 28:25), teaches (John 14:26), witnesses (John 15:26), searches (1 Cor. 2:11), determines (1 Cor. 12:11), intercedes (Rom. 8:26-27), is lied to (Acts 5:3), and can be grieved (Eph. 4:30). Only of a personal being can such things be said.

The divinity of the Spirit appears from the declaration that lying to the Spirit is lying to God (Acts 5:3-4), and from the linking of the Spirit with the Father and the Son in benedictions (2 Cor. 13:14; Rev. 1:4-6) and in the formula of baptism (Matt. 28:19). The Spirit is called "the seven spirits" in Revelation 1:4; 3:1; 4:5; 5:6 partly, it seems, because *seven* is a number signifying divine perfection and partly because the Spirit ministers in his fullness.

The Spirit, then, is "he," not "it," and he must be obeyed, loved, and adored along with the Father and the Son.

Witnessing to Jesus Christ, glorifying him by showing his disciples who and what he is (John 16:7-15), and making them aware of what they are in him (Rom. 8:15-17; Gal. 4:6) is the Paraclete's central ministry. The Spirit enlightens us (Eph. 1:17-18), regenerates us (John 3:5-8), leads us into holiness (Rom. 8:14; Gal. 5:16-18), transforms us (2 Cor. 3:18; Gal. 5:22-23), gives us assurance (Rom. 8:16), and gifts us for ministry (1 Cor. 12:4-11). All God's work in us, touching our hearts, our characters, and our conduct, is done by the Spirit, though aspects of it are

144

sometimes ascribed to the Father and the Son, whose executive the Spirit is.

The Spirit's full Paraclete ministry began on Pentecost morning, following Jesus' ascension (Acts 2:1-4). John the Baptist had foretold that Jesus would baptize in the Spirit (Mark 1:8; John 1:33), according to the Old Testament promise of an outpouring of God's Spirit in the last days (Joel 2:28-32; cf. Jer. 31:31-34), and Jesus had repeated the promise (Acts 1:4-5). The significance of Pentecost morning was twofold: it marked the opening of the final era of world history before Christ's return, and, as compared with the Old Testament era, it marked a tremendous enhancing of the Spirit's ministry and of the experience of being alive to God.

Jesus' disciples were evidently Spirit-born believers prior to Pentecost, so their Spirit-baptism, which brought power to their life and ministry (Acts 1:8), was not the start of their spiritual experience. For all who have come to faith since Pentecost morning, however, beginning with the Pentecost converts themselves, the receiving of the Spirit in full new-covenant blessing has been aspect of their conversion and new birth (Acts 2:37; Rom. 8:9; 1 Cor. 12:13). All capacities for service that subsequently appear in a Christian's life should be seen as flowing from this initial Spirit-baptism, which vitally unites the sinner to the risen Christ.

SALVATION

JESUS RESCUES HIS PEOPLE FROM SIN

*Salvation is found in no one else, for there is
no other name under heaven given to men
by which we must be saved.*

ACTS 4:12

✝ The master theme of the Christian gospel is salvation. *Salvation* is a picture-word of wide application
that expresses the idea of rescue from jeopardy and misery
into a state of safety. The gospel proclaims that the God
who saved Israel from Egypt, Jonah from the fish's belly,
the psalmist from death, and the soldiers from drowning
(Exod. 15:2; Jon. 2:9; Ps. 116:6; Acts 27:31), saves all who
trust Christ from sin and sin's consequences.

As these earthly deliverances were wholly God's work,
and not instances of people saving themselves with God's
help, so it is with salvation from sin and death. "For it is
by grace you have been saved, through faith—and this not
from yourselves, it [either faith as such or salvation and
faith together] is the gift of God" (Eph. 2:8). "Salvation
comes from the LORD" (Jon. 2:9).

What are believers saved from? From their former position under the wrath of God, the dominion of sin, and
the power of death (Rom. 1:18; 3:9; 5:21); from their
natural condition of being mastered by the world, the
flesh, and the devil (John 8:23-24; Rom. 8:7-8; 1 John

5:19); from the fears that a sinful life engenders (Rom. 8:15; 2 Tim. 1:7; Heb. 2:14-15), and from the many vicious habits that were part of it (Eph. 4:17-24; 1 Thess. 4:3-8; Titus 2:11–3:6).

How are believers saved from these things? Through Christ, and in Christ. The Father is as concerned to exalt the Son as he is to rescue the lost (John 5:19-23; Phil. 2:9-11; Col. 1:15-18; Heb. 1:4-14), and it is as true to say that the elect were appointed for Christ the beloved Son as it is to say that Christ was appointed for the beloved elect (Matt. 3:17; 17:5; Col. 1:13; 3:12; 1 Pet. 1:20; 1 John 4:9-10).

Our salvation involves, first, Christ dying for us and, second, Christ living in us (John 15:4; 17:26; Col. 1:27) and we living in Christ, united with him in his death and risen life (Rom. 6:3-10; Col. 2:12, 20; 3:1). This vital union, which is sustained by the Spirit from the divine side and by faith from our side, and which is formed in and through our new birth, presupposes covenantal union in the sense of our eternal election in Christ (Eph. 1:4-6). Jesus was foreordained to be our representative head and substitutionary sin-bearer (1 Pet. 1:18-20; cf. Matt. 1:21), and we were chosen to be effectually called, conformed to his image, and glorified by the Spirit's power (Rom. 8:11, 29-30).

Believers are saved from sin and death, but what are they saved for? To live for time and eternity in love to God—Father, Son, and Spirit—and to their neighbors. The source of love for God is knowledge of God's redeeming love for us, and the evidence of love for God is neighbor-love (1 John 4:19-21). God's purpose, here and hereafter, is to keep expressing his love in Christ to us, and our goal must be to keep expressing our love to the three Persons of the one God by worship and service in Christ. The life of love and adoration is our hope of glory, our salvation now, and our happiness forever.

ELECTION

GOD CHOOSES HIS OWN

For [God] says to Moses, "I will have mercy on whom I have mercy, and I will have compassion on whom I have compassion." It does not, therefore, depend on man's desire or effort, but on God's mercy.

ROMANS 9:15, 16

✝ The verb *elect* means "to select, or choose out." The biblical doctrine of election is that before Creation God selected out of the human race, foreseen as fallen, those whom he would redeem, bring to faith, justify, and glorify in and through Jesus Christ (Rom. 8:28-39; Eph. 1:3-14; 2 Thess. 2:13-14; 2 Tim. 1:9-10). This divine choice is an expression of free and sovereign grace, for it is unconstrained and unconditional, not merited by anything in those who are its subjects. God owes sinners no mercy of any kind, only condemnation; so it is a wonder, and matter for endless praise, that he should choose to save any of us; and doubly so when his choice involved the giving of his own Son to suffer as sin-bearer for the elect (Rom. 8:32).

The doctrine of election, like every truth about God, involves mystery and sometimes stirs controversy. But in Scripture it is a pastoral doctrine, brought in to help Christians see how great is the grace that saves them, and to move them to humility, confidence, joy, praise, faithfulness, and holiness in response. It is the family secret of the children of God. We do not know who else he has chosen among those who do not yet believe, nor why it was his good pleasure to choose us in particular. What we do know is, first, that had we not been chosen for life we would not be believers now (for only the elect are brought to faith), and, second, that as elect believers we may rely on God to finish in us the good work that he started (1 Cor. 1:8-9; Phil. 1:6; 1 Thess. 5:23-24; 2 Tim. 1:12; 4:18). Knowledge of one's election thus brings comfort and joy.

Peter tells us we should be "eager to make [our] calling and election sure" (2 Pet. 1:10)—that is, certain to us. Election is known by its fruits. Paul knew the election of the Thessalonians from their faith, hope, and love, the inward and outward transformation of their lives that the gospel had brought about (1 Thess. 1:3-6). The more that the qualities to which Peter has been exhorting his readers appear in our lives (goodness, knowledge, self-control, perseverance, godliness, brotherly kindness, love: 2 Pet. 1:5-7), the surer of our own election we are entitled to be.

The elect are, from one standpoint, the Father's gift to the Son (John 6:39; 10:29; 17:2, 24). Jesus testifies that he came into this world specifically to save them (John 6:37-40; 10:14-16, 26-29; 15:16; 17:6-26; Eph. 5:25-27), and any account of his mission must emphasize this.

Reprobation is the name given to God's eternal decision regarding those sinners whom he has not chosen for life. His decision is in essence a decision not to change them, as the elect are destined to be changed, but to leave them to sin as in their hearts they already want to do, and finally to judge them as they deserve for what they have done.

When in particular instances God gives them over to their sins (i.e., removes restraints on their doing the disobedient things they desire), this is itself the beginning of judgment. It is called "hardening" (Rom. 9:18; 11:25; cf. Ps. 81:12; Rom. 1:24, 26, 28), and it inevitably leads to greater guilt.

Reprobation is a biblical reality (Rom. 9:14-24; 1 Pet. 2:8), but not one that bears directly on Christian behavior. The reprobates are faceless so far as Christians are concerned, and it is not for us to try to identify them. Rather, we should live in light of the certainty that anyone may be saved if he or she will but repent and put faith in Christ.

We should view all persons that we meet as possibly being numbered among the elect.

EFFECTUAL CALLING
GOD DRAWS HIS PEOPLE TO HIMSELF

*. . . From the beginning God chose you to be
saved through the sanctifying work of the
Spirit and through belief in the truth.
He called you to this through our gospel,
that you might share in the glory
of our Lord Jesus Christ.*

2 THESSALONIANS 2:13-14

✚ *Effectual calling* is a sixteenth-century English phrase that became the title of chapter X of the 1647 Westminster Confession. The chapter begins thus:

All those whom God hath predestinated unto life, and those only, he is pleased, in his appointed and accepted time, effectually to call, by his Word and Spirit, out of that state of sin and death, in which they are by nature, to grace and salvation, by Jesus Christ; enlightening their minds spiritually and savingly to understand the things of God, taking away their heart of stone and giving unto them a heart of flesh; renewing their wills, and, by his almighty power, determining them to that which is good, and effectually drawing them to Jesus Christ: yet so, as they come most freely, being made willing by his grace.

What is being spoken of here is the many-sided reality of Christian conversion, involving illumination, regeneration, faith, and repentance. It is being analyzed as a sovereign work of God, "effectually" (i.e., effectively) performed by the power of the Holy Spirit. The concept corresponds to Paul's use of the verb *call* (meaning "bring to faith") and *called* (meaning "converted") in Romans 1:6; 8:28, 30; 9:24; 1 Corinthians 1:24, 26; 7:18, 21; Galatians 1:15; Ephesians 4:1, 4; and 2 Thessalonians 2:14, and contrasts with the idea of a merely external and ineffective invitation, as found in Matthew 22:14.

Original sin renders all human beings naturally dead (unresponsive) to God, but in effectual calling God quickens the dead. As the outward call of God to faith in Christ is communicated through the reading, preaching, and explaining of the contents of the Bible, the Holy Spirit enlightens and renews the heart of elect sinners so that they understand the gospel and embrace it as truth from God, and God in Christ becomes to them an object of desire and affection. Being now regenerate and able by the use of their freed will to choose God and the good, they turn away from their former pattern of living to receive Jesus Christ as Lord and Savior and to start a new life with him.

ILLUMINATION
THE HOLY SPIRIT GIVES SPIRITUAL UNDERSTANDING

The man without the Spirit does not accept
the things that come from the Spirit of God,
for they are foolishness to him, and he cannot
understand them, because they are
spiritually discerned.

1 CORINTHIANS 2:14

✚ The knowledge of divine things to which Christians are called is more than a formal acquaintance with biblical words and Christian ideas. It is a realizing of the reality and relevance of those activities of the triune God to which Scripture testifies. Such awareness is natural to none, familiar with Christian ideas though they may be (like "the man without the Spirit" in 1 Cor. 2:14 who cannot receive what Christians tell him, or the blind leaders of the blind of whom Jesus speaks so caustically in Matt. 15:14, or like Paul himself before Christ met him on the Damascus road). Only the Holy Spirit, searcher of the deep things of God (1 Cor. 2:10), can bring about this realization in our sin-darkened minds and hearts. That is why it is called "spiritual understanding" (*spiritual* means "Spirit-given," Col. 1:9; cf. Luke 24:25; 1 John 5:20). Those who, along with sound verbal instruction, "have an anointing from the Holy One . . . know the truth" (1 John 2:20).

The work of the Spirit in imparting this knowledge is called "illumination," or enlightening. It is not a giving of new revelation, but a work within us that enables us to grasp and to love the revelation that is there before us in the biblical text as heard and read, and as explained by teachers and writers. Sin in our mental and moral system clouds our minds and wills so that we miss and resist the force of Scripture. God seems to us remote to the point of unreality, and in the face of God's truth we are dull and apathetic. The Spirit, however, opens and unveils our minds and attunes our hearts so that we understand (Eph. 1:17-18; 3:18-19; 2 Cor. 3:14-16; 4:6). As by inspiration he provided Scripture truth for us, so now by illumination he interprets it to us. Illumination is thus the applying of God's revealed truth to our hearts, so that we grasp as reality for ourselves what the sacred text sets forth.

Illumination, which is a lifelong ministry of the Holy Spirit to Christians, starts before conversion with a growing grasp of the truth about Jesus and a growing sense of being measured and exposed by it. Jesus said that the Spirit would "convict the world" of the sin of not believing in him, of the fact that he was in the right with God the Father (as his welcome back to heaven proved), and of the reality of judgment both here and hereafter (John 16:8-11). This threefold conviction is still God's means of making sin repulsive and Christ adorable in the eyes of persons who previously loved sin and cared nothing for the divine Savior.

The way to benefit fully from the Spirit's ministry of illumination is by serious Bible study, serious prayer, and serious response in obedience to whatever truths one has been shown already. This corresponds to Luther's dictum that three things make a theologian: *oratio* (prayer), *meditatio* (thinking in God's presence about the text), and *tentatio* (trial, the struggle for biblical fidelity in the face of pressure to disregard what Scripture says).

REGENERATION

THE CHRISTIAN IS BORN AGAIN

*In reply Jesus declared, "I tell you the truth,
no one can see the kingdom of God
unless he is born again."*

JOHN 3:3

✝ Regeneration is a New Testament concept that grew, it seems, out of a parabolic picture-phrase that Jesus used to show Nicodemus the inwardness and depth of the change that even religious Jews must undergo if they were ever to see and enter the kingdom of God, and so have eternal life (John 3:3-15). Jesus pictured the change as being "born again."

The concept is of God renovating the heart, the core of a person's being, by implanting a new principle of desire, purpose, and action, a dispositional dynamic that finds expression in positive response to the gospel and its Christ. Jesus' phrase "born of water and the Spirit" (John 3:5) harks back to Ezekiel 36:25-27, where God is pictured as symbolically cleansing persons from sin's pollution (by water) and bestowing a "new heart" by putting his Spirit within them. Because this is so explicit, Jesus chides Nicodemus, "Israel's teacher," for not understanding how new birth happens (John 3:9-10). Jesus' point throughout is that there is no exercise of faith in himself as the supernatural Savior, no repentance, and no true discipleship apart from this new birth.

Elsewhere John teaches that belief in the Incarnation and Atonement, with faith and love, holiness and righteousness, is the fruit and proof that one is born of God (1 John 2:29; 3:9; 4:7; 5:1, 4). It thus appears that as there is no conversion without new birth, so there is no new birth without conversion.

Though infant regeneration can be a reality when God so purposes (Luke 1:15, 41-44), the ordinary context of new birth is one of effectual calling—that is, confrontation with the gospel and illumination as to its truth and significance as a message from God to oneself. Regeneration is always the decisive element in effectual calling.

Regeneration is monergistic: that is, entirely the work of God the Holy Spirit. It raises the elect among the spiritually dead to new life in Christ (Eph. 2:1-10). Regeneration is a transition from spiritual death to spiritual life, and conscious, intentional, active faith in Christ is its immediate fruit, not its immediate cause. Regeneration is the work of what Augustine called "prevenient" grace, the grace that precedes our outgoings of heart toward God.

WORKS

GOOD WORKS ARE AN EXPRESSION OF FAITH

*You see that a person is justified by what he
does and not by faith alone.*

JAMES 2:24

✚ In the New Testament, faith (believing trust, or
trustful belief, based on testimony received as from
God) is crucially important, for it is the means or instrumental cause of salvation. It is by faith that Christians are
justified before God (Rom. 3:26; 4:1-5; Gal. 2:16), live
their lives (literally "walk," 2 Cor. 5:7), and sustain their
hope (Heb. 10:35–12:3).

Faith cannot be defined in subjective terms, as a confident and optimistic mind-set, or in passive terms, as acqui-
escent orthodoxy or confidence in God without
commitment to God. Faith is an object-oriented response,
shaped by that which is trusted, namely God himself,
God's promises, and Jesus Christ, all as set forth in the
Scriptures. And faith is a whole-souled response, involving
mind, heart, will, and affections. Older Reformed theology analyzed faith as *notitia* ("knowledge," i.e., acquaintance with the content of the gospel), plus *assensus*
("agreement," i.e., recognition that the gospel is true),
plus *fiducia* ("trust and reliance," i.e., personal dependence
on the grace of Father, Son, and Spirit for salvation, with

thankful cessation of all attempts to save oneself by establishing one's own righteousness: Rom. 4:5; 10:3). Without *fiducia* there is no faith, but without *notitia* and *assensus* there can be no *fiducia* (Rom. 10:14).

God's gift of faith is a fruit of applicatory illumination by the Holy Spirit, and it ordinarily has in it some measure of conscious assurance through the witnessing of the Spirit (Rom. 8:15-17). Calvin defined faith as "a firm and sure knowledge of the divine favor towards us, founded on the truth of a free promise in Christ, and revealed to our minds and sealed on our hearts by the Holy Spirit."

Justification by works (things we have done) is the heresy of legalism. Justification, as Luther insisted, is by faith only ("faith apart from observing the law," Rom. 3:28), because it is in Christ and by Christ only, and depends on what he is as distinct from what we are. But if "good works" (activities of serving God and others) do not follow from our profession of faith, we are as yet believing only from the head, not from the heart: in other words, justifying faith (*fiducia*) is not yet ours. The truth is that, though we are justified by faith alone, the faith that justifies is never alone. It produces moral fruit; it expresses itself "through love" (Gal. 5:6); it transforms one's way of living; it begets virtue. This is not only because holiness is commanded, but also because the regenerate heart, of which *fiducia* is the expression, desires holiness and can find full contentment only in seeking it.

When James says that faith without works is dead (i.e., a corpse), he is using the word *faith* in the limited sense of *notitia* plus *assensus*, which is how those he addresses were using it. When he says that one is justified by what one does, not by faith alone, he means by "justified" "proved genuine; vindicated from the suspicion of being a hypocrite and a fraud." James is making the point that barren orthodoxy saves no one (James 2:14-26). Paul would have agreed, and James's whole letter shows him agreeing with Paul that faith must change one's life. Paul denounces the idea of salvation by dead works; James rejects salvation by dead faith.

Though the believer's works do not merit salvation and always have something imperfect about them (Rom. 7:13-20; Gal. 5:17), in their character as expressions of the love and fidelity that faith calls forth they are the basis on which God promises rewards in heaven (Phil. 3:12-14; 2 Tim. 4:7-8). For God thus to reward us according to our works is, as Augustine noted, his gracious crowning of his own gracious gifts.

REPENTANCE
A CHRISTIAN CHANGES RADICALLY

*. . . I preached that they should repent and
turn to God and prove their repentance
by their deeds.*

ACTS 26:20

✝ The New Testament word for repentance means
changing one's mind so that one's views, values,
goals, and ways are changed and one's whole life is lived
differently. The change is radical, both inwardly and out-
wardly; mind and judgment, will and affections, behavior
and life-style, motives and purposes, are all involved. Repenting means starting to live a new life.

The call to repent was the first and fundamental summons in the preaching of John the Baptist (Matt. 3:2),
Jesus (Matt. 4:17), the Twelve (Mark 6:12), Peter at Pentecost (Acts 2:38), Paul to the Gentiles (Acts 17:30; 26:20),
and the glorified Christ to five of the seven churches in
Asia (Rev. 2:5, 16, 22; 3:3, 19). It was part of Jesus' sum-
mary of the gospel that was to be taken to the world (Luke
24:47). It corresponds to the constant summons of the Old
Testament prophets to Israel to return to the God from
whom they had strayed (e.g., Jer. 23:22; 25:4-5; Zech.
1:3-6). Repentance is always set forth as the path to remission of sins and restoration to God's favor, impenitence as
the road to ruin (e.g., Luke 13:1-8).

162

Repentance is a fruit of faith, which is itself a fruit of regeneration. But in actual life, repentance is inseparable from faith, being the negative aspect (faith is the positive aspect) of turning to Christ as Lord and Savior. The idea that there can be saving faith without repentance, and that one can be justified by embracing Christ as Savior while refusing him as Lord, is a destructive delusion. True faith acknowledges Christ as what he truly is, our God-appointed king as well as our God-given priest, and true trust in him as Savior will express itself in submission to him as Lord also. To refuse this is to seek justification through an impenitent faith, which is no faith.

In repentance, says the Westminster Confession,

a sinner, out of the sight and sense not only of the danger, but also the filthiness and odiousness of his sins, as contrary to the holy nature, and righteous law of God; and upon the apprehension of his mercy in Christ to such as are penitent; so grieves for, and hates his sins, as to turn from them all unto God, purposing and endeavoring to walk with him in all ways of his commandments. (XV.2)

This statement highlights the fact that incomplete repentance, sometimes called "attrition" (remorse, self-reproach, and sorrow for sin generated by fear of punishment, without any wish or resolve to forsake sinning) is insufficient. True repentance is "contrition," as modeled by David in Psalm 51, having at its heart a serious purpose of sinning no more but of living henceforth a life that will show one's repentance to be full and real (Luke 3:8; Acts 26:20). Repenting of any vice means going in the opposite direction, to practice the virtues most directly opposed to it.

JUSTIFICATION
SALVATION IS BY GRACE
THROUGH FAITH

Clearly no one is justified before God
by the law, because,
"The righteous will live by faith."

GALATIANS 3:11

✚ The doctrine of justification, the storm center of the Reformation, was a major concern of the apostle Paul. For him it was the heart of the gospel (Rom. 1:17; 3:21–5:21; Gal. 2:15–5:1) shaping both his message (Acts 13:38-39) and his devotion and spiritual life (2 Cor. 5:13-21; Phil. 3:4-14). Though other New Testament writers affirm the same doctrine in substance, the terms in which Protestants have affirmed and defended it for almost five centuries are drawn primarily from Paul.

Justification is a judicial act of God pardoning sinners (wicked and ungodly persons, Rom. 4:5; 3:9-24), accepting them as just, and so putting permanently right their previously estranged relationship with himself. This justifying sentence is God's gift of righteousness (Rom. 5:15-17), his bestowal of a status of acceptance for Jesus' sake (2 Cor. 5:21).

God's justifying judgment seems strange, for pronouncing sinners righteous may appear to be precisely the unjust action on the judge's part that God's own law forbade

(Deut. 25:1; Prov. 17:15). Yet it is in fact a just judgment, for its basis is the righteousness of Jesus Christ who as "the last Adam" (1 Cor. 15:45), our representative head acting on our behalf, obeyed the law that bound us and endured the retribution for lawlessness that was our due and so (to use a medieval technical term) "merited" our justification. So we are justified justly, on the basis of justice done (Rom. 3:25-26) and Christ's righteousness reckoned to our account (Rom. 5:18-19).

God's justifying decision is the judgment of the Last Day, declaring where we shall spend eternity, brought forward into the present and pronounced here and now. It is the last judgment that will ever be passed on our destiny; God will never go back on it, however much Satan may appeal against God's verdict (Zech. 3:1; Rev. 12:10; Rom. 8:33-34). To be justified is to be eternally secure (Rom. 5:1-5; 8:30).

The necessary means, or instrumental cause, of justification is personal faith in Jesus Christ as crucified Savior and risen Lord (Rom. 4:23-25; 10:8-13). This is because the meritorious ground of our justification is entirely in Christ. As we give ourselves in faith to Jesus, Jesus gives us his gift of righteousness, so that in the very act of "closing with Christ," as older Reformed teachers put it, we receive divine pardon and acceptance which we could not otherwise have (Gal. 2:15-16; 3:24).

Official Roman Catholic theology includes sanctification in the definition of justification, which it sees as a process rather than a single decisive event, and affirms that while faith contributes to our acceptance with God, our works of satisfaction and merit contribute too. Rome sees baptism, viewed as a channel of sanctifying grace, as the primary instrumental cause of justification, and the sacrament of penance, whereby congruous merit is achieved through works of satisfaction, as the supplementary restorative cause whenever the grace of God's initial acceptance is lost through mortal sin. Congruous, as distinct from condign, merit means merit that it is fitting, though not absolutely necessary, for God to reward by a fresh flow of sanctifying grace. On the Roman Catholic view, therefore, believers save themselves with the help of the grace that flows from Christ through the church's sacramental system, and in this life no sense of confidence in God's grace can ordinarily be had. Such teaching is a far cry from that of Paul.

ADOPTION

GOD MAKES HIS PEOPLE
HIS CHILDREN

*But when the fullness of time had come,
God sent his Son, born of a woman,
born under the law . . . so that we might
receive adoption as children.*

GALATIANS 4:4-5 (NRSV)

✝ Paul teaches that the gift of justification (i.e., present acceptance by God as the world's Judge) brings
with it the status of sonship by adoption (i.e., permanent
intimacy with God as one's heavenly Father, Gal. 3:26;
4:4-7). In Paul's world, adoption was ordinarily of young
adult males of good character to become heirs and maintain the family name of the childless rich. Paul, however,
proclaims God's gracious adoption of persons of bad character to become "heirs of God and co-heirs with Christ"
(Rom. 8:17).

Justification is the basic blessing, on which adoption is
founded; adoption is the crowning blessing, to which
justification clears the way. Adopted status belongs to all
who receive Christ (John 1:12). The adopted status of
believers means that in and through Christ God loves
them as he loves his only-begotten Son and will share with
them all the glory that is Christ's now (Rom. 8:17, 38-39).
Here and now, believers are under God's fatherly care and

discipline (Matt. 6:26; Heb. 12:5-11) and are directed, especially by Jesus, to live their whole lives in light of the knowledge that God is their Father in heaven. They are to pray to him as such (Matt. 6:5-13), imitate him as such (Matt. 5:44-48; 6:12, 14-15; 18:21-35; Eph. 4:32–5:2), and trust him as such (Matt. 6:25-34), thus expressing the filial instinct that the Holy Spirit has implanted in them (Rom. 8:15-17; Gal. 4:6).

Adoption and regeneration accompany each other as two aspects of the salvation that Christ brings (John 1:12-13), but they are to be distinguished. Adoption is the bestowal of a relationship, while regeneration is the transformation of our moral nature. Yet the link is evident; God wants his children, whom he loves, to bear his character, and takes action accordingly.

SANCTIFICATION

THE CHRISTIAN GROWS IN GRACE

Do you not know that the wicked will not inherit the kingdom of God? . . . And that is what some of you were. But you were washed, you were sanctified, you were justified in the name of the Lord Jesus Christ and by the Spirit of our God.

1 CORINTHIANS 6:9, 11

✝ Sanctification, says the Westminster Shorter Catechism (Q.35), is "the work of God's free grace, whereby we are renewed in the whole man after the image of God, and are enabled more and more to die unto sin, and live unto righteousness." The concept is not of sin being totally eradicated (that is to claim too much) or merely counteracted (that is to say too little), but of a divinely wrought character change freeing us from sinful habits and forming in us Christlike affections, dispositions, and virtues.

Sanctification is an ongoing transformation within a maintained consecration, and it engenders real righteousness within the frame of relational holiness. Relational sanctification, the state of being permanently set apart for God, flows from the cross, where God through Christ purchased and claimed us for himself (Acts 20:28; 26:18; Heb. 10:10). Moral renovation, whereby we are increasingly changed from what we once were, flows from the agency of the indwelling Holy Spirit (Rom. 8:13; 12:1-2; 1 Cor. 6:11, 19-20; 2 Cor. 3:18; Eph. 4:22-24; 1 Thess. 5:23; 2 Thess. 2:13; Heb. 13:20-21). God calls his children to sanctity and graciously gives what he commands (1 Thess. 4:4; 5:23).

Regeneration is birth; sanctification is growth. In regeneration, God implants desires that were not there before: desire for God, for holiness, and for the hallowing and glorifying of God's name in this world; desire to pray, worship, love, serve, honor, and please God; desire to show love and bring benefit to others. In sanctification, the Holy Spirit "works in you to will and to act" according to God's purpose; what he does is prompt you to "work out your salvation" (i.e., express it in action) by fulfilling these new desires (Phil. 2:12-13). Christians become increasingly Christlike as the moral profile of Jesus (the "fruit of the Spirit") is progressively formed in them (2 Cor. 3:18; Gal. 4:19; 5:22-25). Paul's use of *glory* in 2 Corinthians 3:18 shows that for him sanctification of character is glorification begun. Then the physical transformation that gives us a body like Christ's, one that will match our totally transformed character and be a perfect means of expressing it, will be glorification completed (Phil. 3:20-21; 1 Cor. 15:49-53).

Regeneration was a momentary monergistic act of quickening the spiritually dead. As such, it was God's work alone. Sanctification, however, is in one sense synergistic—it is an ongoing cooperative process in which regenerate persons, alive to God and freed from sin's dominion (Rom. 6:11, 14-18), are required to exert themselves in sustained obedience. God's method of sanctification is neither activism (self-reliant activity) nor apathy (God-reliant passivity), but God-dependent effort (2 Cor. 7:1;

Phil. 3:10-14; Heb. 12:14). Knowing that without Christ's enabling we can do nothing, morally speaking, as we should, and that he is ready to strengthen us for all that we have to do (Phil. 4:13), we "stay put" (remain, abide) in Christ, asking for his help constantly—and we receive it (Col. 1:11; 1 Tim. 1:12; 2 Tim. 1:7; 2:1).

The standard to which God's work of sanctifying his saints is directed is his own revealed moral law, as expounded and modeled by Christ himself. Christ's love, humility, and patience under pressure are to be consciously imitated (Eph. 5:2; Phil. 2:5-11; 1 Pet. 2:21), for a Christlike spirit and attitude are part of what law-keeping involves.

Believers find within themselves contrary urgings. The Spirit sustains their regenerate desires and purposes; their fallen, Adamic instincts (the "flesh") which, though dethroned, are not yet destroyed, constantly distract them from doing God's will and allure them along paths that lead to death (Gal. 5:16-17; James 1:14-15). To clarify the relationship between the law and sin, Paul analyzes in a personal and dramatic way the sense of impotence for complete law-keeping, and the enslavement to behavior one dislikes, that the Spirit-flesh tension produces (Rom. 7:14-25). This conflict and frustration will be with Christians as long as they are in the body. Yet by watching and praying against temptation, and cultivating opposite virtues, they may through the Spirit's help "mortify" (i.e., drain the life out of, weaken as a means of killing) particular bad habits, and in that sense more and more die unto sin (Rom. 8:13; Col. 3:5). They will experience many particular deliverances and victories in their unending battle with sin, while never being exposed to temptations that are impossible to resist (1 Cor. 10:13).

LIBERTY

SALVATION BRINGS FREEDOM

It is for freedom that Christ has set us free.
Stand firm, then, and do not let yourselves
be burdened again by a yoke of slavery.

GALATIANS 5:1

✝ The New Testament sees salvation in Christ as liberation and the Christian life as one of liberty—Christ has freed us for freedom (Gal. 5:1; John 8:32, 36). Christ's liberating action is not a matter of socio-politico-economic improvement, as is sometimes suggested today, but relates to the following three points:

First, Christians have been set free from the law as a system of salvation. Being justified by faith in Christ, they are no longer under God's law, but under his grace (Rom. 3:19; 6:14-15; Gal. 3:23-25). This means that their standing with God (the "peace" and "access" of Rom. 5:1-2) rests wholly on the fact that they have been accepted and adopted in Christ. It does not, nor ever will it, depend on what they do; it will never be imperiled by what they fail to do. They live, and as long as they are in this world will live, not by being perfect, but by being forgiven.

All natural religion, then, is negated, for the natural instinct of fallen man, as expressed in every form of religion that the world has ever devised, is to suppose that one gains and keeps a right relationship with ultimate reality (whether conceived as a personal God or in other terms) by disciplines of law observance, right ritual, and asceticism. This is how the world's faiths prescribe the establishing of one's own righteousness—the very thing Paul saw unbelieving Jews trying to do (Rom. 10:3). Paul's experience had taught him that this is a hopeless enterprise. No human performance is ever good enough, for there are always wrong desires in the heart, along with a lack of right ones, regardless of how correct one's outward motions are (Rom. 7:7-11; cf. Phil. 3:6), and it is at the heart that God looks first.

All the law can do is arouse, expose, and condemn the sin that permeates our moral makeup, and so make us aware of its reality, depth, and guilt (Rom. 3:19; 1 Cor. 15:56; Gal. 3:10). So the futility of treating the law as a covenant of works, and seeking righteousness by it, becomes plain (Gal. 3:10-12; 4:21-31), as does the misery of not knowing what else to do. This is the bondage to the law from which Christ sets us free.

Second, Christians have been set free from sin's domination (John 8:34-36; Rom. 6:14-23). They have been supernaturally regenerated and made alive to God through union with Christ in his death and risen life (Rom. 6:3-11), and this means that the deepest desire of their heart now is to serve God by practicing righteousness (Rom. 6:18, 22). Sin's domination involved not only constant acts of disobedience, but also a constant lack of zeal for law-keeping, rising sometimes to positive resentment and hatred toward the law. Now, however, being changed in heart, motivated by gratitude for acceptance through free grace, and energized by the Holy Spirit, they "serve in the new way of the Spirit, and not in the old way of the written code" (Rom. 7:6). This means that their attempts at obedience are now joyful and integrated in a way that was never true before. Sin rules them no longer. In this respect, too, they have been liberated from bondage.

Third, Christians have been set free from the superstition that treats matter and physical pleasure as intrinsically evil. Against this idea, Paul insists that Christians are free to enjoy as God's good gifts all created things and the pleasures that they yield (1 Tim. 4:1-5), provided only that we do not transgress the moral law in our enjoyments or hinder our own spiritual well-being or that of others (1 Cor. 6:12-13; 8:7-13). The Reformers renewed this emphasis against various forms of medieval legalism.

LEGALISM

WORKING FOR GOD'S FAVOR FORFEITS IT

. . . Do not do what they do, for they do not practice what they preach. They tie up heavy loads and put them on men's shoulders, but they themselves are not willing to lift a finger to move them. Everything they do is done for men to see . . .

MATTHEW 23:3-5

✝ The New Testament views Christian obedience as the practice of "good deeds" (works). Christians are to be "rich in good deeds" (1 Tim. 6:18; cf. Matt. 5:16; Eph. 2:10; 2 Tim. 3:17; Titus 2:7, 14; 3:8, 14). A good deed is one done (a) according to the right standard (God's revealed will, i.e., his moral law); (b) from a right motive (the love to God and others that marks the regenerate heart); (c) with a right purpose (pleasing and glorifying God, honoring Christ, advancing his kingdom, and benefiting one's neighbor).

Legalism is a distortion of obedience that can never produce truly good works. Its first fault is that it skews motive and purpose, seeing good deeds as essentially ways to earn more of God's favor than one has at the moment. Its second fault is arrogance. Belief that one's labor earns God's favor begets contempt for those who do not labor in

175

the same way. Its third fault is lovelessness in that its self-advancing purpose squeezes humble kindness and creative compassion out of the heart.

In the New Testament we meet both Pharisaic and Judaizing legalism. The Pharisees thought that their status as children of Abraham made God's pleasure in them possible, and that their formalized daily law-keeping, down to minutest details, would make it actual. The Judaizers viewed Gentile evangelism as a form of proselytizing for Judaism; they believed that the Gentile believer in Christ must go on to become a Jew by circumcision and observance of the festal calendar and ritual law, and that thus he would gain increased favor with God. Jesus attacked the Pharisees; Paul, the Judaizers.

The Pharisees were formalists, focusing entirely on the externals of action, disregarding motives and purposes, and reducing life to mechanical rule-keeping. They thought themselves faithful law-keepers although (a) they majored in minors, neglecting what matters most (Matt. 23:23-24); (b) their casuistry negated the law's spirit and aim (Matt. 15:3-9; 23:16-24); (c) they treated traditions of practice as part of God's authoritative law, thus binding consciences where God had left them free (Mark 2:16–3:6; 7:1-8); (d) they were hypocrites at heart, angling for man's approval all the time (Luke 20:45-47; Matt. 6:1-8; 23:2-7). Jesus was very sharp with them on these points.

In Galatians, Paul condemns the Judaizers' "Christ-plus" message as obscuring and indeed denying the all-sufficiency of the grace revealed in Jesus (Gal. 3:1-3; 4:21; 5:2-6). In Colossians, he conducts a similar polemic against a similar "Christ-plus" formula for "fullness" (i.e., spiritual completion: Col. 2:8-23). Any "plus" that requires us to take action in order to add to what Christ has given us is a reversion to legalism and, in truth, an insult to Christ.

So far, then, from enriching our relationship with God, as it seeks to do, legalism in all its forms does the opposite. It puts that relationship in jeopardy and, by stopping us focusing on Christ, it starves our souls while feeding our pride. Legalistic religion in all its forms should be avoided like the plague.

ANTINOMIANISM
WE ARE NOT SET FREE TO SIN

*Dear children, do not let anyone lead you
astray. He who does what is right is
righteous, just as he [Christ] is righteous.*

1 JOHN 3:7

✝ *Antinomianism*, which means being "anti-law," is a
name for several views that have denied that God's
law in Scripture should directly control the Christian's
life.

Dualistic antinomianism appears in the Gnostic heretics against whom Jude and Peter wrote (Jude 4-19; 2 Pet.
2). This view sees salvation as for the soul only, and bodily
behavior as irrelevant both to God's interest and to the
soul's health, so one may behave riotously and it will not
matter.

Spirit-centered antinomianism puts such trust in the
Holy Spirit's inward prompting as to deny any need to be
taught by the law how to live. Freedom from the law as a
way of salvation is assumed to bring with it freedom from
the law as a guide to conduct. In the first 150 years of the
Reformation era this kind of antinomianism often threat-
ened, and Paul's insistence that a truly spiritual person
acknowledges the authority of God's Word through
Christ's apostles (1 Cor. 14:37; cf. 7:40) suggests that the

Spirit-obsessed Corinthian church was in the grip of the same mind-set.

Christ-centered antinomianism argues that God sees no sin in believers, because they are in Christ, who kept the law for them, and therefore what they actually do makes no difference, provided that they keep believing. But 1 John 1:8–2:1 (expounding 1:7) and 3:4-10 point in a different direction, showing that it is not possible to be in Christ and at the same time to embrace sin as a way of life.

Dispensational antinomianism holds that keeping the moral law is at no stage necessary for Christians, since we live under a dispensation of grace, not of law. Romans 3:31 and 1 Corinthians 6:9-11 clearly show, however, that law-keeping is a continuing obligation for Christians. "I am not free from God's law but am under Christ's law," says Paul (1 Cor. 9:21).

Dialectical antinomianism, as in Barth and Brunner, denies that biblical law is God's direct command and affirms that the Bible's imperative statements trigger the Word of the Spirit, which when it comes may or may not correspond exactly to what is written. The inadequacy of the neo-orthodox view of biblical authority, which explains the inspiration of Scripture in terms of the Bible's instrumentality as a channel for God's present-day utterances to his people, is evident here.

Situationist antinomianism says that a motive and intention of love is all that God now requires of Christians, and the commands of the Decalogue and other ethical parts of Scripture, for all that they are ascribed to God directly, are mere rules of thumb for loving, rules that love may at any time disregard. But Romans 13:8-10, to which this view appeals, teaches that without love as a motive these specific commands cannot be fulfilled. Once more an unacceptably weak view of Scripture surfaces.

It must be stressed that the moral law, as crystallized in the Decalogue and opened up in the ethical teaching of both Testaments, is one coherent law, given to be a code of practice for God's people in every age. In addition, repentance means resolving henceforth to seek God's help in keeping that law. The Spirit is given to empower law-keeping and make us more and more like Christ, the archetypal law-keeper (Matt. 5:17). This law-keeping is in fact the fulfilling of our human nature, and Scripture holds out no hope of salvation for any who, whatever their profession of faith, do not seek to turn from sin to righteousness (1 Cor. 6:9-11; Rev. 21:8).

LOVE

LOVING IS BASIC TO
CHRISTIAN BEHAVIOR

*Love is patient, love is kind. It does not envy,
it does not boast, it is not proud. It is not
rude, it is not self-seeking, it is not easily
angered, it keeps no record of wrongs. Love
does not delight in evil but rejoices with the
truth. It always protects, always trusts,
always hopes, always perseveres.*

1 CORINTHIANS 13:4-7

✝ New Testament Christianity is essentially response
to the revelation of the Creator as a God of love.
God is a tripersonal Being who so loves ungodly humans
that the Father has given the Son, the Son has given his
life, and Father and Son together now give the Spirit to
save sinners from unimaginable misery and lead them into
unimaginable glory. Believing in and being overwhelmed
by this amazing reality of divine love generates and sustains the love to God and neighbor that Christ's two great
commandments require (Matt. 22:35-40). Our love is to
express our gratitude for God's gracious love to us, and to
be modeled on it (Eph. 4:32–5:2; 1 John 3:16).

The hallmark of Christian life is thus Christian love.
The measure and test of love to God is wholehearted and
unqualified obedience (1 John 5:3; John 14:15, 21, 23); the
measure and test of love to our neighbors is laying down

our lives for them (1 John 3:16; cf. John 15:12-13). This sacrificial love involves giving, spending, and impoverishing ourselves up to the limit for their well-being. Jesus' story of the Samaritan's kindness to the hated Jew stands as his model definition of neighbor-love (Luke 10:25-37).

Neighbor-love is profiled in 1 Corinthians 13:4-8. Its total lack of self-concern is breathtaking. Neighbor-love seeks the neighbor's good, and the true measure of it is how much it gives to that end.

Love is a principle of action rather than of emotion. It is a purpose of honoring and benefiting the other party. It is a matter of doing things for people out of compassion for their need, whether or not we feel personal affection for them. It is by their active love to one another that Jesus' disciples are to be recognized (John 13:34-35).

HOPE

HOPING IS BASIC TO THE CHRISTIAN OUTLOOK

*For everything that was written in the past
was written to teach us, so that through
endurance and the encouragement of the
Scriptures we might have hope.*

ROMANS 15:4

✝ Living between the two comings of Christ, Christians are to look backward and forward: back to the manger, the cross, and the empty tomb, whereby salvation was won for them; forward to their meeting with Christ beyond this world, their personal resurrection, and the joy of being with their Savior in glory forever. New Testament devotion is consistently oriented to this hope; Christ is "our hope" (1 Tim. 1:1) and we serve "the God of hope" (Rom. 15:13). Faith itself is defined as "being sure of what we hope for" (Heb. 11:1), and Christian commitment is defined as having "fled to take hold of . . . this hope as an anchor for the soul" (Heb. 6:18-19). When Jesus directed his disciples to lay up treasure in heaven, because "where your treasure is, there your heart will be also" (Matt. 6:21), he was saying in effect, as Peter was later to say, "set your hope fully on the grace to be given you when Jesus Christ is revealed" (1 Pet. 1:13).

An ethic of hope pervades the New Testament. It is an

ethic of pilgrimage: one should see oneself in this world as a stranger traveling home (1 Pet. 2:11; Heb. 11:13). It is an ethic of purity: everyone who really hopes to be like Jesus when he appears "purifies himself, just as he is pure" (1 John 3:3). It is an ethic of preparedness: we should be ready to leave this world for a closer relationship with Christ our Lord at any time when the summons comes (2 Cor. 5:6-8; Phil. 1:21-24; cf. Luke 12:15-21). It is an ethic of patience: "if we hope for what we do not yet have, we wait for it patiently" (Rom. 8:25; cf. 5:1-5, where the Greek word for "patience" is translated "perseverance" to bring out its nuance of stubborn persistence in face of pressures). And it is an ethic of power: the hope gives strength and confidence, energizing effort for running the race, fighting the good fight, and enduring the "light and momentary troubles" (2 Cor. 4:17) that still remain before we go home (Rom. 8:18; 15:13; 2 Tim. 4:7-8).

Though the Christian life is regularly marked more by suffering than by triumph (1 Cor. 4:8-13; 2 Cor. 4:7-18; Acts 14:22), our hope is sure and our mood should be one of unquenchable confidence: we are on the victory side.

ENTERPRISE

A CHRISTIAN LIVES TO PLEASE GOD

*. . . We are not trying to please men
but God, who tests our hearts.*

1 THESSALONIANS 2:4

✝ It is a familiar truth that every Christian's life-pur-
pose must be to glorify God. This is the believer's
official calling. Everything we say and do, all our obedience to God's commands, all our relationships with others,
all the use we make of the gifts, talents, and opportunities
that God gives us, all our enduring of adverse situations
and human hostility, must be so managed as to give God
honor and praise for his goodness to those on whom he
sets his love (1 Cor. 10:31; cf. Matt. 5:16; Eph. 3:10; Col.
3:17).

Equally important is the truth that every Christian's
full-time employment must be to please God. This may be
properly described as the Christian's personal calling.
Jesus did not live to please himself, nor may we (John 8:29;
Rom. 15:1-3). Pleasing God in everything must be our
goal (2 Cor. 5:9; Col. 1:10; 1 Thess. 2:4; 4:1). Faith (Heb.
11:5-6), praise (Ps. 69:30-31), generosity (Phil. 4:18; Heb.
13:16), obedience to divinely instituted authority (Col.
3:20), and single-mindedness in Christian service (2 Tim.
2:4) combine to form the prescribed way to do it. God

both enables us for this kind of living and takes pleasure in our practice of it. It is his regular procedure in sovereign grace to give what he commands and delight in the result (Heb. 13:21; cf. Phil. 2:12-13).

From the life-controlling summons to please God, we learn the precise sense in which true godliness is both relational and creative. God relates to Christians not only as Father to child but also as Friend to friend. Abraham was called God's friend (2 Chron. 20:7; Isa. 41:8; James 2:23); Christ calls his disciples his friends (Luke 12:4; John 15:14). The measure of God's grace is that he makes friends with sinners; the measure of the Christian's godliness is that one seeks to please one's heavenly Friend, just as spouses seek to please each other in order to show their love (1 Cor. 7:32-35). Christianity is a love affair, and godliness is in essence a matter of expressing grateful, adoring love by seeking to please.

Creativity is part of God's image in man, and it is meant to find expression in an enterprising style of life as we look for ways to show gratitude to God. Love will always ask whether more can be done to please, and more neighbor-love, more service of other's needs, will always be a major part of the answer (1 John 3:11-18). If our plans for pleasing God involve risk, we should remember that Jesus' parable of the talents commends those who risked their money in the market and condemns the practitioner of timid inaction (Matt. 25:14-30).

PRAYER

CHRISTIANS PRACTICE
FELLOWSHIP WITH GOD

*He said to them, "When you pray, say:
'Father, hallowed be your name, your
kingdom come. Give us each day our daily
bread. Forgive us our sins, for we also
forgive everyone who sins against us. And
lead us not into temptation.'"*

LUKE 11:2-4

✝ God made us and has redeemed us for fellowship
with himself, and that is what prayer is. God speaks
to us in and through the contents of the Bible, which the
Holy Spirit opens up and applies to us and enables us to
understand. We then speak to God about himself, and
ourselves, and people in his world, shaping what we say as
response to what he has said. This unique form of two-way
conversation continues as long as life lasts.

The Bible teaches and exemplifies prayer as a fourfold
activity, to be performed by God's people individually
both in private (Matt. 6:5-8) and in company with each
other (Acts 1:14; 4:24). Adoration and praise are to be
expressed; contrite confession of sin is to be made and
forgiveness sought; thanks for benefits received are to be
offered; and petitions and supplications for ourselves and
others are to be voiced. The Lord's Prayer (Matt. 6:9-13;

187

Luke 11:2-4) embodies adoration, petition, and confession; the Psalter consists of models of all four elements of prayer.

Petition, in which the persons praying humbly acknowledge their need and express themselves as trustfully depending on God to meet it out of his sovereign resources of wisdom and goodness, is the dimension of prayer that is most constantly highlighted in the Bible (e.g., Gen. 18:16-33; Exod. 32:31–33:17; Ezra 9:5-15; Neh. 1:5-11; 4:4-5, 9; 6:9, 14; Dan. 9:4-19; John 17; James 5:16-18; Matt. 7:7-11; John 16:23-24; Eph. 6:18-20; 1 John 5:14-16). Petition, along with the other modes of prayer, should ordinarily be directed to the Father, as the Lord's Prayer shows, but Christ may be called on for salvation and healing, as in the days of his flesh (Rom. 10:8-13; 2 Cor. 12:7-9), and the Holy Spirit for grace and peace (Rev. 1:4). It cannot be wrong to present petitions to God as triune or to request any spiritual blessing from any one of the three Persons, but there is wisdom in following the New Testament pattern.

Jesus teaches that petition to the Father is to be made in his name (John 14:13-14; 15:16; 16:23-24). This means invoking his mediation, as the one who secures our access to the Father, and looking to him for support, as our intercessor in the Father's presence. We can only, however, look to him for support when what we ask accords with God's revealed will (1 John 5:14) and our own motives in asking are right (James 4:3).

Jesus teaches that we may properly press God hard with fervent persistence when we bring needs to him (Luke 11:5-13; 18:1-8), and that he will answer such prayer in positive terms. But we must remember that God, who knows what is best in a way that we do not, may deny our specific requests as to how the needs should be met. If he does, however, it is because he has something better to give than what we asked for, as was the case when Christ denied Paul healing for the thorn in his flesh (2 Cor. 12:7-9). To say "Your will be done," surrendering one's own expressed preference to the Father's wisdom as Jesus did in Gethsemane (Matt. 26:39-44), is the most explicit way of expressing faith in the goodness of what God has planned.

There is no tension or inconsistency between the teaching of Scripture on God's sovereign foreordination of all things and on the efficacy of prayer. God foreordains the means as well as the end, and our prayer is foreordained as the means whereby he brings his sovereign will to pass.

Christians who pray to God sincerely, with reverence and humility, with a sense of privilege and a pure (i.e., purified, penitent) heart, will find in themselves a Spirit-given filial instinct prompting prayer to and trust in their heavenly Father (Gal. 4:6; Rom. 8:15), and a desire to pray that outruns their uncertainty as to what thoughts they should express (Rom. 8:26-27). The mysterious reality of the Holy Spirit's help in prayer becomes known only to those who actually pray.

OATHS AND VOWS
CHRISTIANS MUST BE TRUTHFUL

"We will give it back," they said. "And we will not demand anything more from them. We will do as you say."
Then I summoned the priests and made the nobles and officials take an oath to do what they had promised. I also shook out the folds of my robe and said, "In this way may God shake out of his house and possessions every man who does not keep this promise. So may such a man be shaken out and emptied!"
At this the whole assembly said, "Amen," and praised the LORD.
And the people did as they had promised.

NEHEMIAH 5:12-13

✝ Truth in relationships, especially between Christians, is divinely commanded (Eph. 4:25; Col. 3:9), and truth-telling is specified as integral to authentic godliness (Ps. 15:1-3). God forbids lying, deception, and malicious misrepresentation (Exod. 20:16; Lev. 19:11). Jesus traces lying back to Satan (John 8:44), and those who, like Satan, lie in order to deceive and damage others are condemned in Scripture as being ungodly in a hateful and horrible way (Pss. 5:9; 12:1-4; 52:2-5; Jer. 9:3-6; Rev. 22:15). One way of acknowledging the dignity of our neighbor, who is God's image-bearer, is to recognize that he or she has a right to the truth. Truth-telling, which shows proper respect for facts, for our neighbor, and for God, thus becomes a fundamental element in true religion and in true love of one's neighbor.

Expounding the ninth commandment, God's prohibition of false witness (Exod. 20:16), in terms of the principle that the negative implies the positive (i.e., the commandment requires whatever is needed to avoid what it forbids), the Westminster Larger Catechism (Q.144) says:

The duties required are, the preserving and promoting of truth between man and man, and the good name of our neighbor, as well as our own; appearing and standing for the truth; and from the heart, sincerely, freely, clearly, and fully, speaking the truth, and only the truth, in matters of judgment and justice, and in all other things whatsoever.

Oaths are solemn declarations that invoke God as a witness of one's statements and promises, inviting him to punish should one be lying. Scripture approves oath-taking as appropriate on solemn occasions (Gen. 24:1-9; Ezra 10:5; Neh. 5:12; cf. 2 Cor. 1:23; Heb. 6:13-17), though at the time of the Reformation the Anabaptists declined the practice as part of their rejection of involvement in the life of the secular world. They appealed to Jesus' condemnation of oaths devised and designed to deceive as if it were a rejection of oath-taking as such rather than a call for honest speech and a warning against the temptation to use words that give a false impression, with manipulation and exploitation as one's real purpose (Matt. 5:33-37; cf. James 5:12).

Vows to God are the devotional equivalent of oaths and must be treated with equal seriousness (Deut. 21:23; Eccles. 5:4-6). What one swears or vows to do must at all costs be done (Ps. 15:4; cf. Josh. 9:15-18). God requires us to take seriously not only his words but our own as well. However, "no man may vow to do anything forbidden in the Word of God, or what would hinder any duty therein commanded" (Westminster Confession XXII.7).

THE KINDGOM OF GOD

CHRISTIANS MUST MANIFEST KINGDOM LIFE

Once, having been asked by the Pharisees when the kingdom of God would come, Jesus replied, "The kingdom of God does not come with your careful observation, nor will people say, 'Here it is,' or 'There it is,' because the kingdom of God is within you."

LUKE 17:20-21

✝ The theme of the kingdom of God runs through both Testaments, focusing God's purpose for world history. In Old Testament times God declared that he would exercise his kingship (his sovereignty, Dan. 4:34-35) by setting up his kingdom (his rule or reign over people's lives and circumstances) under his chosen king (the Davidic Messiah, Isa. 9:6-7) in a golden age of blessing. This kingdom came with Jesus the Messiah as a worldwide relational reality, existing wherever the lordship of Jesus is acknowledged in repentance, faith, and new obedience. Jesus, the Spirit-anointed, Spirit-filled ruler-designate (Luke 3:21-22; 4:1, 14, 18-21, 32-36, 41), died, rose, ascended, and is now enthroned in heaven as ruler over all things (Matt. 28:18; Col. 1:13), King of kings and Lord of lords (Rev. 17:14; 19:16). The golden age of blessing is an era of present spiritual benefit (salvation from sin and fellowship with God) leading to a future state of unmixed joy in a reconstructed universe. The kingdom is present in its beginnings though future in its fullness; in one sense it is here already, but in the richest sense it is still to come (Luke 11:20; 16:16; 17:21; 22:16, 18, 29-30).

The kingdom came as not only mercy but also judgment, just as John the Baptist, its forerunner, had said it would (Matt. 3:1-12). Those who obediently received Jesus' Word and put their destiny in his hands found mercy, while the Jewish leadership, which would not do this, was judged. Strictly speaking, the Jewish leaders were self-judged, for they chose to live in darkness by retreating from the Savior (John 3:17-20).

The task of the church is to make the invisible kingdom visible through faithful Christian living and witness-bearing. The gospel of Christ is still the gospel of the kingdom (Matt. 4:23; 24:14; Acts 20:25; 28:23, 31), the good news of righteousness, peace, and joy in the Holy Spirit through entering a disciple's relationship to the living Lord (Rom. 14:17). The church must make its message credible by manifesting the reality of kingdom life.

The coming of the kingdom meant a new stage in God's redemptive-historical program. The Messiah arrived, redeemed, and withdrew to his throne with a promise that he would come again. All that was typical, temporary, and imperfect in the God-given arrangements for Israel's communion with himself became a thing of the past. God's Israel, Abraham's seed, was redefined as the company of believers in Jesus (Gal. 3:16, 26-29). The Spirit was poured out, and a new way of life, namely life in Christ and with Christ, became a reality of this world. Thus the new internationalism of global church fellowship and global evangelism was born (Eph. 2:11-18; 3:6, 14-15; Rev. 5:9-10; 7:9; Matt. 28:19-20; Col. 1:28-29). Although these were great changes, none of them meant that a new set of moral standards emerged, as is sometimes supposed. The moral law for Christians, the law of God's present kingdom, is the law found in the Ten Commandments and the prophets, now applied to the new situation. Jesus has not abolished that law but has merely filled out its meaning (Matt. 5:17-48).

APOSTLES

JESUS' REPRESENTATIVES
EXERCISED HIS AUTHORITY

Then they drew lots,
and the lot fell to Matthias;
so he was added to the eleven apostles.

ACTS 1:26

✝ Although the Gospels call the same people "disciples" and "apostles" (Mark 3:7, 14, 20), the terms are not synonyms. *Disciple* means "pupil, learner"; *apostle* means "emissary, representative," in the sense of one who is sent with the full authority of the sender. The "twelve apostles of the Lamb" (Rev. 21:14), as distinct from the apostles ("representatives") of the churches (2 Cor. 8:23) and from the rest of Jesus' disciples, were chosen and sent by Jesus (Mark 3:14) just as Jesus himself, "the apostle . . . whom we confess" (Heb. 3:1), was chosen and sent by the Father (1 Pet. 1:20). Just as rejecting Jesus is rejecting the Father, so rejecting the apostles is rejecting Jesus (Luke 10:16).

The New Testament shows the apostles functioning as evangelists, church planters in the sense of community founders, and pastors, just as Jesus himself had functioned in these three roles during his earthly ministry. As Jesus claimed the Father's divine authority for his words (John 12:49-50; 14:24), so the apostles claimed Christ's divine authority for theirs (1 Thess. 2:13; 2 Thess. 3:6; cf. 1 Cor. 2:12-13; 14:37).

Acts 1:15-26 shows us the church before Pentecost prayerfully asking Christ through the casting of a lot to choose a successor to Judas. Whether they were right to do this, and Paul was Christ's thirteenth apostle, or whether Paul was Christ's intended replacement for Judas and the choice of Matthias was a mistake, is not clear in Acts; Luke himself may not have known. Paul, the "apostle to the Gentiles" (Rom. 11:13; Gal. 2:8), who announces himself as an apostle in the opening words of most of his letters, insisted that, because he had seen Christ on the Damascus road and been commissioned by him (Acts 26:16-18), he was as truly a witness to Jesus' resurrection (which an apostle was to be, Acts 1:21-22; 10:41-42) as were the others. James, Peter, and John accepted Paul into apostolic partnership (Gal. 2:9), and God confirmed his status by the signs of an apostle (miracles and manifestations, 2 Cor. 12:12; Heb. 2:3-4) and by the fruitfulness of his ministry (1 Cor. 9:2).

The apostles were agents of God's revelation of the truths that would become the Christian rule of faith and life. As such, and through Christ's appointment of them as his authorized representatives (2 Cor. 10:8; 13:10), the apostles exercised a unique and functional authority in the infant church. There are no apostles today, though some Christians fulfill ministries that are in particular ways apostolic in style. No new canonical revelation is currently being given; apostolic teaching authority resides in the canonical Scriptures, of which the apostles' own writings are the core and the key. The absence of new revelation does not, however, put the contemporary church at any disadvantage compared with the church of apostolic days, for the Holy Spirit interprets and applies these Scriptures to God's people continually.

CHURCH

GOD PLANTS HIS PEOPLE IN A NEW COMMUNITY

Consequently, you are no longer foreigners and aliens, but fellow citizens with God's people and members of God's household, built on the foundation of the apostles and prophets, with Christ Jesus himself as the chief cornerstone. In him the whole building is joined together and rises to become a holy temple in the Lord. And in him you too are being built together to become a dwelling in which God lives by his Spirit.

EPHESIANS 2:19-22

✝ The church (Greek: *ecclesia,* meaning "assembly") exists in, through, and because of Jesus Christ. Thus it is a distinctive New Testament reality. Yet it is at the same time a continuation, through a new phase of redemptive history, of Israel, the seed of Abraham, God's covenant people of Old Testament times. The differences between the church and Israel are rooted in the newness of the covenant by which God and his people are bound to each other. The new covenant under which the church lives (1 Cor. 11:25; Heb. 8:7-13) is a new form of the relationship whereby God says to a chosen community, "I will be your God; you shall be my people" (Exod. 6:7; Jer. 31:33). Both the continuity and the discontinuity between

Israel and the church reflect this change in the form of the covenant, which took place at Christ's coming.

The new features of the new covenant are as follows: First, the Old Testament priests, sacrifices, and sanctuary are superseded by the mediation of Jesus, the crucified, risen, and reigning God-man (Heb. 1–10), in whom believers now find their identity as the seed of Abraham and the people of God (Gal. 3:29; 1 Pet. 2:4-10).

Second, the ethnic exclusivism of the old covenant (Deut. 7:6; Ps. 147:19-20) is replaced by the inclusion in Christ on equal terms of believers from all nations (Eph. 2–3; Rev. 5:9-10).

Third, the Spirit is poured out both on each Christian and on the church, so that fellowship with Christ (1 John 1:3), ministry from Christ (John 12:32; 14:18; Eph. 2:17), and foretastes of heaven (2 Cor. 1:22; Eph. 1:14) become realities of churchly experience.

The unbelief of most Jews (Rom. 9–11) led to a situation depicted by Paul as God breaking off the natural branches of his olive tree (the historical covenant community) and replacing them with wild olive shoots (Rom. 11:17-24). The predominantly Gentile character of the church is due not to the terms of the new covenant but to Jewish rejection of them, and Paul taught that this will one day be reversed (Rom. 11:15, 23-31).

The New Testament defines the church in terms of the fulfillment of Old Testament hopes and patterns through a relationship to all three Persons of the Godhead, brought about by the mediatorial ministry of Jesus Christ. The church is seen as the family and flock of God (Eph. 2:18; 3:15; 4:6; John 10:16; 1 Pet. 5:2-4), his Israel (Gal. 6:16); the body and bride of Christ (Eph. 1:22-23;

5:25-28; Rev. 19:7; 21:2, 9-27); and the temple of the Holy Spirit (1 Cor. 3:16; cf. Eph. 2:19-22). Those in the church are called the "elect" (chosen), the "saints" (consecrated ones, set apart for God), and the "brothers" (adopted children of God).

Essentially, the church is, was, and always will be a single worshiping community, permanently gathered in the true sanctuary which is the heavenly Jerusalem (Gal. 4:26; Heb. 12:22-24), the place of God's presence. Here all who are alive in Christ, the physically living with the physically dead (i.e., the church militant with the church triumphant) worship continually. In the world, however, this one church appears in the form of local congregations, each one called to fulfill the role of being a microcosm (a small-scale representative sample) of the church as a whole. This explains how it is that for Paul the one church universal is the body of Christ (1 Cor. 12:12-26; Eph. 1:22-23; 3:6; 4:4), and so is the local congregation (1 Cor. 12:27).

It is customary to characterize the church on earth as "one" (because it really is so in Christ, as Eph. 4:3-6 shows, despite the great number of local churches and denominational groupings), "holy" (because it is consecrated to God corporately, as each Christian is individually, Eph. 2:21), "catholic" (because it is worldwide in extent and seeks to hold the fullness of the faith), and "apostolic" (because it is founded on apostolic teaching, Eph. 2:20). All four qualities may be illustrated from Ephesians 2:19-22.

There is a distinction to be drawn between the church as we humans see it and as God alone can see it. This is the historic distinction between the "visible church" and the "invisible church." *Invisible* means, not that we can see no sign of its presence, but that we cannot know (as God, the heart-reader, knows, 2 Tim. 2:19) which of those baptized, professing members of the church as an organized institution are inwardly regenerate and thus belong to the church as a spiritual fellowship of sinners loving their Savior. Jesus taught that in the organized church there would always be people who thought they were Christians and passed as Christians, some indeed becoming ministers, but who were not renewed in heart and would therefore be exposed and rejected at the Judgment (Matt. 7:15-27; 13:24-30, 36-43, 47-50; 25:1-46). The "visible-invisible" distinction is drawn to take account of this. It is not that there are two churches but that the visible community regularly contains imitation Christians whom God knows not to be real (and who could know this for themselves if they would, 2 Cor. 13:5).

The New Testament assumes that all Christians will share in the life of a local church, meeting with it for worship (Heb. 10:25), accepting its nurture and discipline (Matt. 18:15-20; Gal. 6:1), and sharing in its work of witness. Christians disobey God and impoverish themselves by refusing to join with other believers when there is a local congregation that they can belong to.

God does not prescribe for Christian worship in the detailed fashion of Old Testament times, but the New Testament shows clearly what the staple ingredients of corporate Christian worship are, namely, praise ("psalms, hymns, and spiritual songs," Eph. 5:19), prayer, and preaching, with regular administration of the Lord's Supper (Acts 20:7-11). Singing to God's praise was evidently a big thing in the apostolic church, as it has been in all movements of spiritual power ever since: Paul and Barnabas, along with their praying (aloud), sang hymns in the prison in Philippi (Acts 16:25), and the New Testament contains a number of what appear to be hymn fragments (Eph. 5:14; Phil. 2:6-11; 1 Tim. 3:16; and others) while the "new songs" of Revelation are both numerous and exuberant, indeed ecstatic (Rev. 4:8, 11; 5:9-10, 12-13; 7:10, 12; 11:15, 17-18; 12:10-12; 15:3-4; 19:1-8; 21:3-4). Any local church anywhere that is spiritually alive will undoubtedly take its singing, praying, and preaching very seriously indeed, and be jealous for all three.

WORD AND SACRAMENT

HOW A GENUINE CHURCH IS IDENTIFIED

. . . the church in Ephesus . . . the church in Smyrna . . . the church in Pergamum . . . the church in Thyatira . . . the church in Sardis . . . the church in Philadelphia . . . the church in Laodicea . . .

REVELATION 2:1, 8, 12, 18; 3:1, 7, 14

✝ Each local church is an outcrop of the one universal church and will embody the nature of that church as the Father's regenerate family, Christ's ministering body, and a fellowship sustained by the Holy Spirit. The world contains self-styled churches with doubtful or false credentials (e.g., the Unitarian churches and the Mormon church, both of which deny the Trinity). Furthermore, congregations that once held the faith unambiguously have been known to lapse to the point where it is hard to know if they are churches anymore. Discernment is therefore necessary. As they opposed the papacy and separated from the Roman Catholic church, the Reformers needed to determine the marks of the true church. From Scripture, they found the answer in terms of two criteria.

1. *The faithful preaching of the Word of God.* This means that the group in question teaches from Scripture the

essentials of the Christian gospel. Denials of the Trinity, the deity of Christ, the sin-bearing atonement, and justification by faith, for example, link aberrant contemporary groups with the docetic separatists, whose denials of Incarnation and Atonement (1 John 4:1-3) caused John to say, "They did not really belong to us" (1 John 2:19).

2. *The right use of the sacraments.* This means that baptism and the Lord's Supper are seen and explained as setting forth the gospel so as to evoke, confirm, and strengthen faith in Christ. Superstitions that stifle faith by turning the sacraments into magic rites are intolerable. Such superstitions strike at churchly identity in a radical way, as does anything else that obstructs faith in Christ. Reception into the visible church is part of what being baptized means; confirmation of one's place in it is part of what sharing in the Lord's Supper means. Right use of the sacraments involves an element of church discipline whereby professions of faith are tested and public behavior is reviewed.

Ideally, a Christian congregation will exhibit other marks of its identity alongside these minimal two. Luther specified the keys of discipline (Matt. 16:19), an authorized ministry (Acts 14:23; 20:28), public worship (Heb. 10:25), and suffering under the cross (Acts 14:22; 20:29). The Reformed churches specified a functioning system of discipline and have spoken of discipline as a third criterion or mark of the visible church (Titus 1:13; 2:15; 3:10). Charismatics and others today specify the active ministry of every member as another mark of the true church (Eph. 4:7-16).

These additional marks are not, however, essential in the way that the minimal two are. A church that lacks them is certainly deficient, but it would not be true to say that it is not a church at all.

ELDERS

PASTORS MUST CARE
FOR THE CHURCH

*He must hold firmly to the trustworthy
message as it has been taught, so that he can
encourage others by sound doctrine and
refute those who oppose it.*

TITUS 1:9

✝ The apostles told all Christians to watch over each other with loving care and prayer (Gal. 6:1-2; 1 John 3:16-18; 5:16; Heb. 12:15-16), but they also appointed in each congregation guardians, called "elders" (Acts 14:23; Titus 1:5), who would look after the people as shepherds look after sheep (Acts 20:28-31; 1 Pet. 5:1-4), leading them by example (1 Pet. 5:3) away from all that is harmful into all that is good. In virtue of their role, the elders (presbyters: Greek: *presbuteroi*) are also called "shepherds" (Greek: *poimenes*, or "pastors," Eph. 4:11) and overseers (Greek: *episkopoi*, or "bishops," Acts 20:28, cf. v. 17; Titus 1:5, cf. v. 7; 1 Pet. 5:1-2), and are spoken of in other terms that express leadership (Rom. 12:8; 1 Thess. 5:12; Heb. 13:7, 17, 24). The congregation, for its part, is to acknowledge the God-given authority of its leaders and follow the lead they give (Heb. 13:17).

This pattern is already present in the Old Testament, where God is the shepherd of Israel (Ps. 80:1) and kings, prophets, priests, and elders (local rulers) are called to act as his agents in an under-shepherd role (Num. 11:24-30; Deut. 27:1; Ezra 5:5; 6:14; 10:8; Ps. 77:20; Jer. 23:1-4; Ezek. 34; Zech. 11:16-17). In the New Testament, Jesus the Good Shepherd (John 10:11-30) is also the Chief Shepherd (1 Pet. 5:4), and the elders are his subordinates. The apostle Peter calls himself an "elder" under Christ (1 Pet. 5:1), remembering perhaps that spiritual shepherding was the specific task that Jesus gave him when restoring him to ministry (John 21:15-17).

Some though not all elders teach (1 Tim. 5:17; Titus 1:9; Heb. 13:7), and Ephesians 4:11-16 says that Christ gave the church "pastor-teachers" (one class of persons with a dual role) to equip everyone for service through the discovery and development of each person's spiritual gifts (vv. 12-16). In the congregational leadership groups envisaged by the apostles, there may have been teachers who were not elders (2 Tim. 2:2) as well as elders who did not teach and elders who both ruled and taught.

The pastoral role of elders demands mature and stable Christian character and a well-ordered personal life (1 Tim. 3:1-7; Titus 1:5-9). Wholeheartedness and fidelity in eldership ministry will be rewarded (Heb. 13:17; 1 Pet. 5:4; cf. 1 Tim. 4:7-8).

The pastoral responsibilities of the apostles and their deputies, like Timothy and Titus, were wider than those of congregational elders (2 Cor. 11:28; Titus 1:5), while those of congregational deacons (Greek: *diakonoi*, or "servants," perhaps elders' assistants, 1 Tim. 3:8-13; Phil. 1:1) were narrower, with particular responsibility for the ministry of mercy (Acts 6:2-6; Rom. 16:1-2).

Every church needs ministerial functionaries to fulfill the eldership role, and should set in place a wise method of selecting and appointing them.

SACRAMENTS

CHRIST INSTITUTED TWO SEALS
OF GOD'S COVENANT

*[Abraham] . . . received the sign of
circumcision, a seal of the righteousness that
he had by faith while he was still
uncircumcised.*

ROMANS 4:11

✝ Christ instituted two rites that his followers were to observe: baptism, a once-for-all rite of initiation (Matt. 28:19; Gal. 3:27), and the Lord's Supper, a regular rite of remembrance (1 Cor. 11:23-26). These are called "sacraments" in the Western church, "mysteries" in the Eastern Orthodox church, and "ordinances" by some Protestants who see the other two words as tainted with unhelpful associations. Scripture has no category-word for these two rites and their Old Testament counterparts, namely circumcision of males as a rite of initiation (Gen. 17:9-14, 23-27) and the annual Passover as a rite of remembrance (Exod. 12:1-27). Biblical teaching, however, warrants classifying them all together as signs and seals of a covenant relationship with God.

Sacrament is from the Latin word *sacramentum*, meaning a holy rite in general and in particular a soldier's sacred oath of allegiance. Study of the rites themselves yields the concept of a sacrament as a ritual action instituted by

Christ in which signs perceived through the senses set forth to us the grace of God in Christ and the blessings of his covenant. They communicate, seal, and confirm possession of those blessings to believers, who by responsively receiving the sacraments give expression to their faith and allegiance to God. The effect of receiving the sacraments is "to put a visible difference between those that belong unto the church and the rest of the world, and solemnly to engage them to the service of God in Christ, according to his word" (Westminster Confession XXVII.1).

It was a medieval mistake to classify as sacraments five more rites (confirmation, penance, marriage, ordination, and extreme unction). In addition to their not being seals of a covenant relationship with God, they "have not like nature of sacraments with Baptism and the Lord's Supper, for that they have not any visible sign or ceremony ordained of God" (Thirty-Nine Articles XXV).

The sacraments are rightly viewed as means of grace, for God makes them means to faith, using them to strengthen faith's confidence in his promises and to call forth acts of faith for receiving the good gifts signified. The efficacy of the sacraments to this end resides not in the faith or virtue of the minister but in the faithfulness of God, who, having given the signs, is now pleased to use them. Knowing this, Christ and the apostles not only speak of the sign as if it were the thing signified but speak too as if receiving the former is the same as receiving the latter (e.g., Matt. 26:26-28; 1 Cor. 10:15-21; 1 Pet. 3:21-22). As the preaching of the Word makes the gospel audible, so the sacraments make it visible, and God stirs up faith by both means.

Sacraments strengthen faith by correlating Christian

beliefs with the testimony of our senses. The Heidelberg Catechism illustrates this in its answer to Question 75. The key words are *as sure as*.

Christ has commanded me . . . to eat of this broken bread and to drink of this cup in memory of him, and therewith has given assurance: first, that his body was . . . broken on the cross for me, and his blood shed for me, as sure as I see with my eyes the bread . . . broken for me and the cup communicated to me; and, further, that with his crucified body and shed blood he himself feeds and nourishes my soul to eternal life, as sure as I take and taste the bread and cup . . . which are given me as sure tokens of the body and blood of Christ.

Sacraments function as means of grace on the principle that, literally, seeing is (i.e., leads to) believing.

BAPTISM

THIS RITE EXHIBITS UNION WITH CHRIST

Or don't you know that all of us who were baptized into Christ Jesus were baptized into his death? We were therefore buried with him through baptism into death in order that, just as Christ was raised from the dead through the glory of the Father, we too may live a new life.

ROMANS 6:3-4

✚ Christian baptism, which has the form of a ceremonial washing (like John's pre-Christian baptism), is a sign from God that signifies inward cleansing and remission of sins (Acts 22:16; 1 Cor. 6:11; Eph. 5:25-27), Spirit-wrought regeneration and new life (Titus 3:5), and the abiding presence of the Holy Spirit as God's seal testifying and guaranteeing that one will be kept safe in Christ forever (1 Cor. 12:13; Eph. 1:13-14). Baptism carries these meanings because first and fundamentally it signifies union with Christ in his death, burial, and resurrection (Rom. 6:3-7; Col. 2:11-12); and this union with Christ is the source of every element in our salvation (1 John 5:11-12). Receiving the sign in faith assures the persons baptized that God's gift of new life in Christ is freely given to them. At the same time, it commits them to live henceforth in a new way as committed disciples of Jesus. Bap-

212

tism signifies a watershed point in a human life because it signifies a new-creational ingrafting into Christ's risen life.

Christ instructed his disciples to baptize in the name of the Father, the Son, and the Holy Spirit (Matt. 28:19). This means that the covenant relation which baptism formally confers is one of acceptance by, communion with, and commitment to all three Persons of the Godhead. When Paul says that the Israelites were "baptized into Moses" (1 Cor. 10:2), he means that they were put under Moses' control and direction. Thus, baptism into the name of the triune God signifies control and direction by God himself.

The outward sign does not automatically or magically convey the inward blessings that it signifies, and the candidates' professions of faith are not always genuine. Peter had to tell the newly baptized Simon Magus that he was still unrenewed in heart (Acts 8:13-24).

As a sign of a once-for-all event, baptism should be administered to a person only once. Baptism is real and valid if water and the triune name are used, even if it is of an adult whose profession turns out to have been hypocritical. Simon Magus received baptism once, and if he came to real faith later it would have been incorrect to baptize him again.

No prescription of a particular mode of baptism can be found in the New Testament. The command to baptize may be fulfilled by immersion, dipping, or sprinkling; all three modes satisfy the meaning of the Greek verb *baptizo* and the symbolic requirement of passing under, and emerging from, cleansing water.

To baptize believers' babies, in the belief that this accords with God's revealed will, has been the historic practice of most churches. However, the worldwide baptist community, which includes distinguished Reformed thinkers, disputes it.

This links up with the baptist insistence that membership of local congregations is only for those who have publicly professed personal faith: an emphasis often buttressed by the claim that Christ instituted baptism primarily for a public profession of faith, and that such a profession is part of the definition of baptism, so that infant baptism is not really baptism at all. (Therefore baptist churches usually rebaptize as believers persons baptized in infancy who have come to faith; from the baptist standpoint they are still unbaptized.) Reformed theology negates the view that believer-baptism is the only baptism and rejects baptist denials of a place for believers' children in the body of Christ by virtue of their parentage, and thus from birth. These differences about the visible church form the background for all discussions of infant baptism as such.

The case for baptizing believers' infants (a practice that the New Testament neither illustrates nor prescribes nor forbids) rests on the claim that the transition from the "old" to the "new" form of God's covenant that was brought about by the coming of Christ did not affect the principle of family solidarity in the covenant community (i.e., the church, as it is now called). Infants were therefore to be baptized, as Jewish male infants had previously been circumcised, not to confer on them covenant status, but to attest the covenant status that by God's sovereign appointment their parentage had already given them.

In 1 Corinthians 7:14, Paul resolves the question of whether God accepts a marriage in which only one partner has become a Christian by invoking the certainty that the children of such a marriage are relationally and covenantally "holy," that is, are dedicated to and accepted by God in company with their one Christian parent. So the principle of parent-and-child solidarity still stands, as Peter also indicated in his Pentecost sermon (Acts 2:39). But if infants share covenant status with their parent, it is fitting, other things being equal, to give them the sign of that status and of their place in the covenant community, and it would be unfitting for the church to withhold it. This fitness is demonstrated by the fact that when circumcision was the sign of covenant status and community inclusion, God commanded it explicitly (Gen. 17:9-14).

Against this, baptists affirm that (a) circumcision was primarily a sign of Jewish ethnic identity, so the parallel alleged between it and Christian baptism is a mistake; (b) under the new covenant, the requirement of personal faith before baptism is absolute; and (c) practices that Scripture does not explicitly recognize and approve must not be brought into church life.

Certainly, all adult church members should have professed faith personally before the church, and communities that baptize infants provide for this in a rite of confirmation or its equivalent. The Christian nurture of baptist and paedobaptist children will be similar: dedicated to God in infancy, either by baptism or by a dedication rite (which some will see as a dry baptism), they will then be brought up to live for the Lord and led to the point of publicly professing faith on their own account in confirmation or baptism (which some will see as a wet confirmation). After this they will enjoy full communicant status, unless indeed they come under discipline for some lapse. The ongoing debate is not about nurture but about God's way of defining the church.

THE LORD'S SUPPER

THIS RITE EXHIBITS COMMUNION WITH CHRIST

For I received from the Lord what I also passed on to you: The Lord Jesus, on the night he was betrayed, took bread, and when he had given thanks, he broke it and said, "This is my body, which is for you; do this in remembrance of me." In the same way, after supper he took the cup, saying, "This cup is the new covenant in my blood; do this, whenever you drink it, in remembrance of me." For whenever you eat this bread and drink this cup, you proclaim the Lord's death until he comes.

1 CORINTHIANS 11:23-26

✝ The Lord's Supper is an act of worship taking the form of a ceremonial meal, in which Christ's servants share bread and wine in memory of their crucified Lord and in celebration of the new covenant relationship with God through Christ's death.

Our Lord Jesus, in the night wherein he was betrayed, instituted the sacrament of his body and blood, called the Lord's Supper, to be observed in his church, unto the end of the world, for the perpetual remembrance of the sacrifice of himself in his death; the sealing of all benefits thereof unto true believers, their spiritual nourishment and growth in him, their further encouragement in and to all duties which they owe unto him; and, to be a bond and pledge of their communion with him,

217

and with each other, as members of his mystical body. (West-minster Confession XXIX.1)

The passages dealing with the Supper on which the above statement is based are the four institution narratives (Matt. 26:26-29; Mark 14:22-25; Luke 22:17-20; 1 Cor. 11:23-25) and 1 Corinthians 10:16-21; 11:17-34. Jesus' sermon (John 6:35-58) about himself as the Bread of Life, and the need to feed on him by eating his flesh and drinking his blood, was preached before the Supper existed and is better understood as being about what the Supper signifies (i.e., communion with Christ by faith) than about the Supper itself.

At the time of the Reformation, questions about the nature of Christ's presence in the Supper and the relation of the rite to his atoning death were centers of stormy controversy. On the first question, the Roman Catholic church affirmed (as it still affirms) transubstantiation, defined by the Fourth Lateran Council in 1215. *Transubstantiation* means that the substance of the bread and wine are miraculously transformed into the substance of Christ's body and blood so that they are no longer bread and wine, though they appear to be. Luther modified this, affirming what was later called "consubstantiation" (a term that Luther did not favor), namely, that Christ's body and blood come to be present in, with, and under the form of the bread and wine, which thus become more than bread and wine though not less. The Eastern Orthodox churches and some Anglicans say much the same. Zwingli denied that the glorified Christ, now in heaven, is present in any way that the words *bodily, physically,* or *locally* would fit. Calvin held that though the bread and wine remained unchanged (he agreed with Zwingli that the *is* of "this is my body . . . my blood" means "represents," not "constitutes"), Christ through the Spirit grants worshippers true enjoyment of his personal presence, drawing them into fellowship with himself in heaven (Heb. 12:22-24) in a way that is glorious and very real, though indescribable.

On the second question, all the Reformers insisted that at the table we give thanks to Christ for his finished and accepted work of atonement, rather than repeat, renew, reoffer, re-present, or reactivate it, as the Roman Catholic doctrine of the mass affirms.

The prescribed ritual of the Supper has three levels of meaning for participants. First, it has a *past* reference to Christ's death which we remember. Second, it has a *present* reference to our corporate feeding on him by faith, with implications for how we treat our fellow believers (1 Cor. 11:20-22). Third, it has a *future* reference as we look ahead to Christ's return and are encouraged by the thought of it. Preliminary self-examination, to make sure one's frame of mind is as it should be, is advised (1 Cor. 11:28), and the wisdom of the advice is obvious.

DISCIPLINE

THE CHURCH MUST UPHOLD CHRISTIAN STANDARDS

If your brother sins against you, go and show him his fault, just between the two of you. If he listens to you, you have won your brother over. But if he will not listen, take one or two others along, so that "every matter may be established by the testimony of two or three witnesses." If he refuses to listen to them, tell it to the church; and if he refuses to listen even to the church, treat him as you would a pagan or a tax collector.

MATTHEW 18:15-17

✝ The Christian concept of discipline has the same breadth as the Latin word *disciplina*, which signifies the whole range of nurturing, instructional, and training procedures that disciple-making requires. When Reformed theology highlights the importance of church discipline, insisting that there is no spiritual health without it and that it is a vital mark of a true church, more is in view than judicial processes against immoral persons and heretics. Only where the personal disciplines of learning and devotion, worship and fellowship, righteousness and service are being steadily taught in a context of care and accountability (Matt. 28:20; John 21:15-17; 2 Tim. 2:14-26; Titus 2; Heb. 13:17) is there a meaningful place for judicial correctives. The New Testament clearly shows, however, that in that context judicial correctives have a significant place in the maturing of churches and individuals (1 Cor. 5:1-13; 2 Cor. 2:5-11; 2 Thess. 3:6, 14-15; Titus 1:10-14; 3:9-11).

Jesus instituted church discipline by authorizing the apostles to bind and to loose (i.e., prohibit and permit, Matt. 18:18) and to declare sins remitted or retained (John 20:23). The "keys of the kingdom," first given to Peter and defined as power to bind and loose (Matt. 16:19), have usually been understood as authority to formulate doctrine and impose discipline, an authority now given by Christ to the church in general and to commissioned pastors in particular.

The Westminster Confession declares:

Church censures are necessary, for the reclaiming and gaining of offending brethren, for deterring of others from the like offenses, for purging out of that leaven which might infect the whole lump, for vindicating the honor of Christ, and the holy profession of the gospel, and for preventing the wrath of God, which might justly fall upon the church, if they should suffer his covenant, and the seals thereof [the sacraments] to be profaned by notorious and obstinate offenders. (XXX.3)

Church censures may have to escalate from bare admonition through exclusion from the Lord's Supper to expulsion from the congregation (excommunication), which is described as handing a person over to Satan, the prince of this world (Matt. 18:15-17; 1 Cor. 5:1-5, 11; 1 Tim. 1:20; Titus 3:10-11). Public sins (i.e., those that are open to the whole church's view) should be publicly corrected in the church's presence (1 Tim. 5:20; cf. Gal. 2:11-14). Jesus teaches a procedure for dealing privately with those who have given personal offense, in hope that it will not be necessary to ask for the church's public censure of them (Matt. 18:15-17).

The purpose of church censure in all its forms is not to punish for punishment's sake but to call forth repentance and so recover the straying sheep. Ultimately there is only one sin for which a church member is excommunicated—impenitence. When repentance is apparent, the church is to declare the sin remitted and receive the offender into fellowship once again.

MISSION
CHRIST SENDS THE CHURCH
INTO THE WORLD

Again Jesus said, "Peace be with you! As the Father has sent me, I am sending you."

JOHN 20:21

✝ *Mission* is from the Latin *missio*, which means "sending." The words Jesus spoke to his first disciples in their representative capacity, "As the Father has sent me, I am sending you" (John 20:21; cf. 17:18), still apply. The universal church, and therefore every local congregation and every Christian in it, is sent into the world to fulfill a definite, defined task. Jesus, the church's Lord, has issued marching orders. Individually and corporately, all God's people are now in the world on the king's business.

The appointed task is twofold. First and fundamentally, it is the work of worldwide witness, disciple-making, and church-planting (Matt. 24:14; 28:19-20; Mark 13:10; Luke 24:47-48). Jesus Christ is to be proclaimed everywhere as God incarnate, Lord, and Savior; and God's authoritative invitation to find life through turning to Christ in repentance and faith (Matt. 22:1-10; Luke 14:16-24) is to be delivered to all mankind. The ministry of church-planter Paul, evangelist (so far as strength and circumstances allowed) to the whole world (Rom. 1:14;

223

15:17-29; 1 Cor. 9:19-23; Col. 1:28-29), models this primary commitment.

Second, all Christians, and therefore every congregation of the church on earth, are called to practice deeds of mercy and compassion, a thoroughgoing neighbor-love that responds unstintingly to all forms of human need as they present themselves (Luke 10:25-27; Rom. 12:20-21). Compassion was the inward aspect of the neighbor-love that led Jesus to heal the sick, feed the hungry, and teach the ignorant (Matt. 9:36; 15:32; 20:34; Mark 1:41; Luke 7:13), and those who are new creatures in Christ must be similarly compassionate. Thereby they keep the second great commandment and also give credibility to their proclamation of a Savior who makes sinners into lovers of God and of their fellow human beings. If the exponents of this message do not display its power in their own lives, credibility is destroyed. If they do, credibility is enhanced. This was Jesus' point when he envisaged the sight of the good works of his witnesses leading people to glorify the Father (Matt. 5:16; cf. 1 Pet. 2:11-12). Good works should be visible to back up good words.

Though Jesus anticipated the Gentile mission (Matt. 24:14; John 10:16; 12:32), he saw his earthly ministry as directed to "the lost sheep of Israel" (Matt. 15:24). Paul, the apostle to the Gentiles, always went to Jews first wherever he evangelized (Acts 13:5, 14, 42-48; 14:1; 16:13; 17:1-4, 10; 18:4-7, 19; 19:8-10; 28:17-28; Rom. 1:16; 2:9-10). The right of the Jews to hear the gospel first is a matter of divine appointment (Acts 3:26; 13:26, 46), and evangelistic outreach to Jews should continue to be a priority as the church seeks to fulfill its mission. Christian Jews are free from the ceremonial law but are also free to follow Jewish customs that express their ethnic culture. The long-standing expectation that Jewish Christians will leave behind their Jewish identity rather than rejoice in being "fulfilled" Jews is a cultural prejudice with no biblical basis.

SPIRITUAL GIFTS

THE HOLY SPIRIT EQUIPS
THE CHURCH

But to each one of us grace has been given
as Christ apportioned it. . . . He . . . gave
some to be apostles, some to be prophets, some
to be evangelists, and some to be pastors and
teachers, to prepare God's people for works of
service, so that the body of Christ
may be built up.

EPHESIANS 4:7, 11-12

✝ The New Testament depicts local churches in which some Christians hold formal and official ministerial offices (elder-overseers and deacons, Phil. 1:1), while all fulfill informal serving roles. Every-member ministry in the body of Christ is the New Testament ideal. It is clear that officers who oversee should not restrict the informal ministries but rather should facilitate them (Eph. 4:11-13), just as it is clear that those who minister informally should not be defiant or disruptive but should allow the overseers to direct their ministries in ways that are orderly and edifying (i.e., strengthening and upbuilding, 1 Cor. 14:3-5, 12, 26, 40; Heb. 13:17). The body of Christ grows to maturity in faith and love "as each part does its work" (Eph. 4:16) and fulfills its grace-given form of service (Eph. 4:7, 12).

The word *gift* (literally "donation") appears in connection with spiritual service only in Ephesians 4:7-8. Paul

explains the phrase *he . . . gave gifts to men* as referring to
the ascended Christ giving his church persons called to
and equipped for the ministries of apostle, prophet, evangelist, and pastor-teacher. Also, through the enabling
ministry of these functionaries, Christ is bestowing a
ministry role of one sort or another on every Christian.
Elsewhere (Rom. 12:4-8; 1 Cor. 12–14) Paul calls these
divinely given powers to serve *charismata* (gifts which are
specific manifestations of *charis* or grace, God's active and
creative love, 1 Cor. 12:4), and also *pneumatika* (spiritual
gifts as specific demonstrations of the energy of the Holy
Spirit, God's *pneuma*, 1 Cor. 12:1).

Amid many obscurities and debated questions regarding New Testament *charismata*, three certainties
stand out. First, a spiritual gift is an ability in some
way to express, celebrate, display, and so communicate Christ. We are told that gifts, rightly used, build
up Christians and churches. But only knowledge of
God in Christ builds up, so each *charisma* must be an
ability from Christ to show and share Christ in an
upbuilding way.

Second, gifts are of two types. There are gifts of
speech and of loving, practical helpfulness. In Romans
12:6-8, Paul's list of gifts alternates between the catego-
ries: items one, three, and four (prophecy, teaching, and
exhorting) are gifts of speech; items two, five, six, and
seven (serving, giving, leading, and showing mercy) are
gifts of helpfulness. The alternation implies that no
thought of superiority of one gift over another may
enter in. However much gifts differ as forms of human
activity, all are of equal dignity, and the only question

is whether one properly uses the gift one has (1 Pet. 4:10-11).

Third, no Christian is giftless (1 Cor. 12:7; Eph. 4:7), and it is everyone's responsibility to find, develop, and fully use whatever capacities for service God has given.

MARRIAGE

MATRIMONY IS MEANT TO BE A PERMANENT COVENANT RELATIONSHIP

"I hate divorce," says the LORD
God of Israel. . . .

MALACHI 2:16

✚ Marriage is an exclusive relationship in which a man
and a woman commit themselves to each other in
covenant for life, and on the basis of this solemn vow
become "one flesh" physically (Gen. 2:24; Mal. 2:14; Matt.
19:4-6).

"Marriage was ordained for the mutual help of husband
and wife, for the increase of mankind with a legitimate
issue, and of the church with an holy seed; and for preventing of uncleanness [sexual license and immorality]" (Westminster Confession XXIV.2; Gen. 2:18; 1:28; 1 Cor.
7:2-9). God's ideal for marriage is that the man and the
woman should experience mutual completion (Gen. 2:23)
and share in his creative work of making new people.
Marriage is for all mankind, but it is God's will that his
own people should only marry fellow believers (1 Cor.
7:39; cf. 2 Cor. 6:14; Ezra 9–10; Neh. 13:23-27). Intimacy
at its deepest is impossible when the partners are not
united in faith.

By using Christ's relationship to his church to illustrate

what Christian marriage ought to be, Paul highlights the husband's special responsibility as his wife's leader and protector, and the wife's calling to accept her husband in that role (Eph. 5:21-33). The distinction of roles does not, however, imply that the wife is an inferior person: as God's image-bearers, the husband and the wife have equal dignity and value, and they are to fulfill their role relationship on the basis of a mutual respect that is rooted in recognition of this fact.

God hates divorce (Mal. 2:16), yet he provided a procedure for it that would protect the divorced wife (Deut. 24:1-4); this, said Jesus (Matt. 19:8), was "because your hearts were hard." The natural way to understand his teaching in Matthew 5:31-32 and 19:8-9 is that marital unfaithfulness (the sin of adultery) destroys the marriage covenant and warrants divorce (though reconciliation would be preferable); but he who divorces his wife for any lesser reason becomes guilty of adultery when he remarries and drives her into adultery in her remarriage. In this Jesus is simply stating the principle that all cases of divorce and remarriage involve disruption of God's idea for the sexual relationship. He answered the question, When is divorce lawful? by saying that divorce is always deplorable (Matt. 19:3-6), but he did not deny that hearts continue to be hard; so that divorce, though always in itself an evil, may sometimes be permitted on a lesser-evil basis.

Paul says that one who has become a Christian and then been deserted by an unbelieving partner is not "bound" (1 Cor. 7:15). This evidently means that he or she may regard the relationship as finished. Whether this should be held to confer right of remarriage has been disputed, and Reformed opinion has long been divided on the matter.

The Westminster Confession (XXIV.5-6) states with cautious wisdom what most Reformed Christians, reflecting on the Scriptures quoted above, have down the centuries found themselves agreed on regarding divorce:

In the case of adultery after marriage, it is lawful for the innocent party to sue out [secure] a divorce: and, after the divorce, to marry another, as if the offending party were dead.

Although the corruption of man be such as is apt to study arguments unduly to put asunder those whom God hath joined together in marriage: yet, nothing but adultery, or such wilful desertion as can no way be remedied by the church, or civil magistrate, is cause sufficient of dissolving the bond of marriage: wherein, a public and orderly course of proceeding is to be observed; and the persons concerned in it not left to their own wills, and discretion, in their own case.

THE FAMILY
THE CHRISTIAN HOUSEHOLD
IS A SPIRITUAL UNIT

*Submit to one another out of reverence
for Christ.*

EPHESIANS 5:21

✝ The family (i.e., the household, consisting of parents and children, with or without relatives, friends, and servants in addition) is the oldest and most basic of human institutions. The Bible stresses its importance as a spiritual unit and a training ground for mature adult character.

The family has a built-in authority structure whereby the husband is leader to the wife and the parents are leaders to the children. All leadership is a form of ministry rather than of tyranny, and these domestic leadership roles must be fulfilled in love (Eph. 5:22–6:4; Col. 3:18-21; 1 Pet. 3:1-7). The fourth commandment requires the head of the house to lead his whole family in sabbath-keeping; the fifth requires children to respect and submit to their parents (Exod. 20:8-12; Eph. 6:1-3). Jesus himself set an example in this (Luke 2:51). Later, he fiercely opposed supposed gestures of piety that were really evasions of responsibility toward parents (Mark 7:6-13), and his own last act before he died was to provide for his mother's future (John 19:25-27).

The family is to be a community of teaching and learning about God and godliness. Children must be instructed (Gen. 18:18-19; Deut. 4:9; 6:6-8; 11:18-21; Prov. 22:6; Eph. 6:4) and must be encouraged to take the instruction seriously as a basis for their living (Prov. 1:8; 6:20). Discipline, which means directive and corrective training, is necessary to lead children beyond childish folly to self-controlled wisdom (Prov. 13:24; 19:18; 22:15; 23:13-14; 29:15, 17). Just as there is purposeful, loving discipline in God's family (Prov. 3:11-12; Heb. 12:5-11), so there must be in the human family.

The family is meant to function as a spiritual unit. The Old Testament Passover was a family occasion (Exod. 12:3). Joshua was setting an example when he said, "As for me and my household, we will serve the LORD" (Josh. 24:15). Households became the units of Christian commitment in New Testament times (Acts 11:14; 16:15, 31-33; 1 Cor. 1:16). The fitness of candidates for church office was assessed by observing whether they had led their family well (1 Tim. 3:4-5, 12; Titus 1:6).

The building of strong family life must always be a priority in our service of God.

THE WORLD

CHRISTIANS ARE IN SOCIETY TO SERVE AND TRANSFORM IT

Since you died with Christ to the basic principles of this world, why, as though you still belonged to it, do you submit to its rules: "Do not handle! Do not taste! Do not touch!"? These are all destined to perish with use, because they are based on human commands and teachings.

COLOSSIANS 2:20-22

✝ *World* in the New Testament sometimes means what it means in the Old Testament, namely, this earth, the good natural order that God created. Usually, however, it means mankind as a whole, now fallen into sin and moral disorder and become radically anti-God and evil. Occasionally the two senses seem to blend, so that statements about the world carry the complex nuance of perverse people incurring guilt and shame by their misuse of created things.

Christians are sent into the world by their Lord (John 17:18) to witness to it about God's Christ and his kingdom (Matt. 24:14; cf. Rom. 10:18; Col. 1:6, 23) and to serve its needs. But they are to do so without falling victim to its materialism (Matt. 6:19-24, 32), its unconcern about God and the next life (Luke 12:13-21), and its prideful pursuit of pleasure, profit, and position to the exclusion of everything else (1 John 2:15-17). The world is at present Satan's kingdom (John 14:30; 2 Cor. 4:4; 1 John 5:19; cf. Luke 4:5-7), and the outlook and mind-set of human societies reflect more of the pride seen in Satan than the humility seen in Christ.

Christians, like Christ, are to empathize with people's anxieties and needs in order to serve them and communicate with them effectively. They are to do so, however, on a basis of motivational detachment from this world, through which they are momentarily passing as they travel home to God and in which their single-minded purpose must be to please God (Col. 1:9-12; 1 Pet. 2:11). Monastic withdrawal from this world is not sanctioned (John 17:15), but neither is worldliness (i.e., any internalizing of the earthbound self-absorption of the people of this world: Titus 2:12). Jesus encourages his disciples to match worldly persons' ingenuity in using their resources to further their goals, but he specifies that their proper goals have to do not with earthly security but with heavenly glory (Luke 16:9).

God's first requirement, then, of Christians in this world is that they be different from those around them, observing God's moral absolutes, practicing love, avoiding shameful license, and not losing their dignity as God's image-bearers through any form of irresponsible self-indulgence (Rom. 12:2; Eph. 4:17-24; Col. 3:5-11). A clean break with the world's value-systems and life-styles is called for, as a basis for practicing Christlikeness in positive terms (Eph. 4:25–5:17).

The Christian's appointed task is threefold. The church's main mandate is evangelism (Matt. 28:19-20; Luke 24:46-48), and every Christian must seek by all means to further the conversion of unbelievers. The impact of one's own changed life will be significant here (1 Pet. 2:12). Also, neighbor-love should constantly lead the Christian into deeds of mercy of all sorts. But in addition, Christians are called to fulfill the "cultural mandate" that God gave to mankind at Creation (Gen. 1:28-30; Ps. 8:6-8). Man was made to manage God's world, and this stewardship is part of the human vocation in Christ. It calls for hard work, with God's honor and the good of others as its goal. This is the real Protestant "work ethic." It is essentially a religious discipline, the fulfillment of a divine "calling."

Knowing that God in providential kindness and forbearance continues, in face of human sin, to preserve and enrich his erring world (Acts 14:16-17), Christians are to involve themselves in all forms of lawful human activity, and by doing that in terms of the Christian value system and vision of life they will become salt (a preservative that makes things taste better) and light (an illumination that shows the way to go) in the human community (Matt. 5:13-16). As Christians thus fulfill their vocation, Christianity becomes a transforming cultural force.

THE STATE

CHRISTIANS MUST RESPECT CIVIL GOVERNMENT

*Everyone must submit himself to
the governing authorities, for there is no
authority except that which God has
established. The authorities that exist have
been established by God. Consequently,
he who rebels against the authority
is rebelling against what God has instituted,
and those who do so will bring judgment
on themselves.*

ROMANS 13:1-2

✚ Civil government is a means ordained by God for ruling over communities. It is one of a number of such means, including ministers in the church, parents in the home, and teachers in the school. Each such means has its own sphere of authority under Christ, who now rules the universe on his Father's behalf, and each sphere has to be delimited by reference to the others. In our fallen world these structures of authority are institutions of God's "common grace" (kindly providence), standing as a bulwark against anarchy, the law of the jungle, and the dissolution of ordered society.

Basing itself on Romans 13:1-7 and 1 Peter 2:13-17, the Westminster Confession sets forth the sphere of civil government as follows:

237

God, the supreme Lord and King of all the world, hath or-
dained civil magistrates, to be, under him, over the people, for
his own glory, and the public good; and, to this end, hath
armed them with the power of the sword, for the defence and
encouragement of them that are good, and for the punishment
of evil doers. . . . The civil magistrate may not assume to him-
self the administration of the Word and sacraments, or the
power of the keys of the kingdom of heaven. (XXIII.1, 3)

Because civil government exists for the welfare of the
whole society, God gives it the power of the sword (i.e.,
the lawful use of force to enforce just laws: Rom. 13:4).
Christians must acknowledge this as part of God's order
(Rom. 13:1-2). But civil authorities ought not to use this
power to persecute the adherents or nonadherents of any
particular religion, or to entrench any form of evil.

The state may properly collect taxes for the services it
renders (Matt. 22:15-21; Rom. 13:6-7). But should it for-
bid what God requires or require what God forbids, some
form of civil disobedience, with acceptance of its penal
consequences (thus showing that one recognizes the God-
given authority of governments as such), becomes inescapable (Acts 4:18-31; 5:17-29).

Christians are to urge governments to fulfill their
proper role. They are to pray for, obey, and yet watch over
civil governments (1 Tim. 2:1-4; 1 Pet. 2:13-14), remind-
ing them that God ordained them to rule, protect, and
keep order but not to tyrannize. In a fallen world, in which
power regularly corrupts, democratic institutions that di-
vide executive power among many and make all its holders
answerable to the people ordinarily offer the best hope of
avoiding tyranny and securing justice for all.

PART FOUR

GOD REVEALED AS LORD OF DESTINY

PERSEVERANCE

GOD KEEPS HIS PEOPLE SAFE

And those he predestined, he also called; those
he called, he also justified; those he justified,
he also glorified.

ROMANS 8:30

✝ Let it first be said that in declaring the eternal
security of God's people it is clearer to speak of their
preservation than, as is commonly done, of their perseverance. Perseverance means persistence under discouragement and contrary pressure. The assertion that believers
persevere in faith and obedience despite everything is true,
but the reason is that Jesus Christ through the Spirit
persists in preserving them.

Scripture emphasizes this. John tells us that Jesus
Christ, the Good Shepherd, is under promise to his Father
(John 6:37-40) and to his sheep directly (John 10:28-29) to
keep them so that they never perish. In his high-priestly
prayer before his passion Jesus asked that those whom the
Father had given him (John 17:2, 6, 9, 24) would be
preserved to glory, and it is inconceivable that his prayer,
which still continues (Rom. 8:34; Heb. 7:25), will go
unanswered.

Paul sees the sovereign plan of God for the salvation
of his elect as a unitary whole, of which the glorifying of
the justified is part (Rom. 8:29-30). On this basis he

builds the triumphant peroration of Romans 8:31-39, in which he celebrates the present and future security of the saints in the almighty love of God. Elsewhere he rejoices in the certainty that God will complete the "good work" that he began in the lives of those Paul addresses (Phil. 1:6; cf. 1 Cor. 1:8-9; 1 Thess. 5:23-24; 2 Thess. 3:3; 2 Tim. 1:12; 4:18).

Reformed theology echoes this emphasis. The Westminster Confession declares,

They, whom God hath accepted in his Beloved, effectually called, and sanctified by his Spirit, can neither totally nor finally fall from the state of grace, but shall certainly persevere therein to the end, and be eternally saved. (XVII.1)

The doctrine declares that the regenerate are saved through persevering in faith and Christian living to the end (Heb. 3:6; 6:11; 10:35-39), and that it is God who keeps them persevering. That does not mean that all who ever professed conversion will be saved. False professions are made; short-term enthusiasts fall away (Matt. 13:20-22); many who say to Jesus, "Lord, Lord," will not be acknowledged (Matt. 7:21-23). Only those who show themselves to be regenerate by pursuing heart-holiness and true neighbor-love as they pass through this world are entitled to believe themselves secure in Christ. Persevering in faith and penitence, not just in Christian formalism, is the path to glory. To suppose that believing in perseverance leads to careless living and arrogant presumption is a total misconception.

Sometimes the regenerate backslide and fall into gross sin. But in this they act out of character, do violence to their own new nature, and make themselves deeply miserable, so that eventually they seek and find restoration to righteousness. In retrospect, their lapse seems to them to have been madness. When regenerate believers act in character, they manifest a humble, grateful desire to please the God who saved them; and the knowledge that he is pledged to keep them safe forever simply increases this desire.

UNPARDONABLE SIN

ONLY IMPENITENCE
CANNOT BE FORGIVEN

I tell you the truth, all the sins and
blasphemies of men will be forgiven them.
But whoever blasphemes against the Holy
Spirit will never be forgiven;
he is guilty of an eternal sin.

MARK 3:28-29

✝ When Jesus warned the Pharisees that blasphemy against the Holy Spirit was unpardonable both in this world and in the next (Matt. 12:32; Mark 3:29-30), it was because they were saying that he exorcised demons by being in league with Satan (Beelzebub). His warning revealed his view of their spiritual state.

He could, and later did, pray for the forgiveness of those whose blasphemy against himself was the fruit of ignorance: "Father, forgive them, for they do not know what they are doing" (Luke 23:34). But that was not how he saw the Pharisees.

It is possible for people to be enlightened to the point of knowing inwardly that Jesus is the divine Savior he claims to be, and still not be willing to admit it publicly, because of all the behavioral changes that such an admission would make necessary. It is possible to try to make oneself feel good about one's own moral dishonesty by

244

inventing reasons, no matter how absurd, for not treating Jesus as worthy of one's allegiance. Jesus evidently perceived that in calling him Satan's servant the Pharisees were doing exactly that. They were not ignorant; they were stifling conviction and smothering real if unwelcome knowledge; they were resolutely shutting their eyes to the light and callousing their conscience by calling it darkness. The madness that Jesus exposed in what they were saying (Matt. 12:25-28) was an index of the pressure of conviction that they were feeling; irrational reasoning is a regular sign of conviction being resisted.

By attributing exorcisms wrought through the Holy Spirit (Matt. 12:28) to Satanic power, the Pharisees were blaspheming (speaking impiously) against the Spirit. Such a sin would become unforgivable when the conscience had been so calloused by calling good evil that all sense of the moral glory of Jesus' mighty works (which were in a real sense his credentials: Matt. 11:2-6; John 10:38; 14:11) was destroyed. This hardening of heart against Jesus would preclude any remorse at any stage for having thus blasphemed. But nonexistence of remorse makes repentance impossible, and nonexistence of repentance makes forgiveness impossible.

Callousing one's conscience by dishonest reasonings so as to justify denial of God's power in Christ and rejection of his claims upon one is, then, the formula of the unpardonable sin. Another version of it, this time in professed Christians who fall away from Christ, is described in Hebrews 6:4-8. Christians who fear that they may have committed the unpardonable sin show by their very anxiety that they have not done so. Persons who have committed it are unremorseful and unconcerned; indeed, they are ordinarily unaware of what they have done and to what fate they have sentenced themselves. Jesus saw that the Pharisees were getting close to committing this sin, and he spoke as he did in hope of holding them back from fully lapsing into it.

MORTALITY

CHRISTIANS NEED NOT FEAR DEATH

For to me, to live is Christ and to die is gain.
If I am to go on living in the body, this will mean
fruitful labor for me. Yet what shall I choose?
I do not know! I am torn between the two:
I desire to depart and be with Christ,
which is better by far; but it is more necessary
for you that I remain in the body.

PHILIPPIANS 1:21-24

✝ We do not know how humans would have left this world had there been no Fall; some doubt whether they ever would have done so. But as it is, the separation of body and soul through bodily death, which is both sin's fruit and God's judgment (Gen. 2:17; 3:19, 22; Rom. 5:12; 8:10; 1 Cor. 15:21), is one of life's certainties. This separating of the soul (person) from the body is a sign and emblem of the spiritual separation from God that first brought about physical death (Gen. 2:17; 5:5) and that will be deepened after death for those who leave this world without Christ. Naturally, therefore, death appears as an enemy (1 Cor. 15:26) and a terror (Heb. 2:15).

For Christians the terror of physical death is abolished, though the unpleasantness of dying remains. Jesus, their risen Savior, has himself passed through a more traumatic death than any Christian will ever have to face, and he now lives to support his servants as they move out of this world to the place he has prepared for them in the next world (John 14:2-3). Christians should view their own forthcoming death as an appointment in Jesus' calendar, which he will faithfully keep. Paul could say, "For to me, to live is Christ and to die is gain. . . . I desire to depart and be with Christ, which is better by far" (Phil. 1:21, 23), since "away from the body" will mean "at home with the Lord" (2 Cor. 5:8).

At death the souls of believers (i.e., the believers themselves, as ongoing persons) are made perfect in holiness and enter into the worshiping life of heaven (Heb. 12:22-24). In other words, they are glorified. Some, not believing this, posit a purgatorial discipline after death that is really a further stage of sanctification, progressively purifying the heart and refining the character in preparation for the vision of God. But this belief is neither scriptural nor rational, for if at Christ's coming saints alive on earth will be perfected morally and spiritually in the moment of their bodily transformation (1 Cor. 15:51-54), it is only natural to suppose that the same is done for each believer in the moment of death, when the mortal body is left behind. Others posit unconsciousness (soul sleep) between death and resurrection, but Scripture speaks of conscious relationship, involvements, and enjoyments (Luke 16:22; 23:43; Phil. 1:23; 2 Cor. 5:8; Rev. 6:9-11; 14:13).

Death is decisive for destiny. After death there is no possibility of salvation for the lost (Luke 16:26)—from then on both the godly and the ungodly reap what they sowed in this life (Gal. 6:7-8).

Death is gain for believers (Phil. 1:21) because after death they are closer to Christ. But disembodiment, as such, is not gain; bodies are for expression and experience, and to be without a body is to be limited, indeed impoverished. This is why Paul wants to be "clothed" with his resurrection body (i.e., re-embodied) rather than be "unclothed" (i.e., disembodied, 2 Cor. 5:1-4). To be resurrected for the life of heaven is the true Christian hope. As life in the "intermediate" or "interim" state between death and resurrection is better than the life in this world that preceded it, so the life of resurrection will be better still. It will, in fact, be best. And this is what God has in store for all his children (2 Cor. 5:4-5; Phil. 3:20-21). Hallelujah!

SECOND COMING

JESUS CHRIST WILL RETURN TO THE EARTH IN GLORY

Now, brothers, about times and dates we do not need to write to you, for you know very well that the day of the Lord will come like a thief in the night. While people are saying, "Peace and safety," destruction will come on them suddenly, as labor pains on a pregnant woman, and they will not escape.
But you, brothers, are not in darkness so that this day should surprise you like a thief.

1 THESSALONIANS 5:1-4

✝ The New Testament repeatedly announces that Jesus Christ will one day be back. This will be his "royal visit," his "appearing" and "coming" (Greek: *parousia*). Christ will return to this world in glory. The Savior's second advent will be personal and physical (Matt. 24:44; Acts 1:11; Col. 3:4; 2 Tim. 4:8; Heb. 9:28), visible and triumphant (Mark 8:38; 2 Thess. 1:10; Rev. 1:7). Jesus comes to end history, to raise the dead and judge the world (John 5:28-29), to impart to God's children their final glory (Rom. 8:17-18; Col. 3:4), and to usher in a reconstructed universe (Rom. 8:19-21; 2 Pet. 3:10-13). His execution of this agenda will be the last phase and final triumph of his mediatorial kingdom. Once these things are done, the applying of redemption against Satanic op-

250

position, which was the specific work of the kingdom, will be over. When Paul says that Christ then "hands over the kingdom" and becomes subject to the Father (1 Cor. 15:24-28), he is not implying any diminution in Christ's subsequent honor, but is signifying the completion of the plan for bringing the elect to heaven that the risen Son was enthroned to carry through. The elect in glory, purified and perfected, will forever honor the Lamb as the one who was able to open the book of God's plan for the accomplishing and applying of redemption in history, and make what was planned happen (Rev. 5). In the new Jerusalem, God and the Lamb are enthroned and reign together forever (Rev. 22:1, 3). But this reigning is the ongoing servant-Lord relationship between God and the godly that follows the era of the mediatorial kingdom, rather than the continuation of that kingdom as such.

In 1 Thessalonians 4:16-17 Paul teaches that Christ's coming will take the form of a descent from the sky, heralded by a trumpet fanfare, a shout, and the voice of the archangel. Those who died in Christ will already have been raised and will be with him, and all Christians on earth will be "raptured" (i.e., caught up among the clouds to meet Christ in the air) so that they may at once return to earth with him as part of his triumphant escort. The idea that the rapture takes them out of this world for a period before Christ appears a third time for a second "second coming" has been widely held but lacks scriptural support.

Though some of the details Paul gives have symbolic significance (the trumpet, like a military bugle, demands attention to God's activity, Exod. 19:16, 19; Isa. 27:13; Matt. 24:31; 1 Cor. 15:52; the clouds signify God's active

251

presence, Exod. 19:9, 16; Dan. 7:13; Matt. 24:30; Rev. 1:7), he seems to be speaking literally, and the fact that what he describes is beyond our power to imagine should not stop us from taking his word that this is how it will be.

The New Testament specifies much that will take place between Christ's two comings, but apart from the fall of Jerusalem in A.D. 70 (Luke 21:20, 24) the predictions point to processes rather than single identifiable events and do not yield even an approximate date for Jesus' reappearance. The Gentile world will be summoned to faith (Matt. 24:14); Jews will be brought into the kingdom (Rom. 11:25-29, a passage that may or may not anticipate a national conversion); there will be false prophets and false Christs or antichrists (Matt. 24:5, 24; 1 John 2:18, 22; 4:3). There will be apostasy from the faith and tribulation for the faithful (2 Thess. 2:3; 1 Tim. 4:1; 2 Tim. 3:1-5; Rev. 7:13-14; cf. 3:10). A seemingly unidentifiable "man of lawlessness," about whom Paul had told the Thessalonians in oral teaching that we do not have (2 Thess. 2:5), was or is due to appear (2 Thess. 2:3-12). If the thousand-year period of Revelation 20:1-10 is actually world history between Christ's two comings, there will be a last climactic power struggle of some sort between the world's anti-Christian forces and the people of God (vv. 7-9). No dates, however, can be deduced from this data; the time of Jesus' return remains completely unknown.

The return of Christ will have the same significance for Christians who will be alive when it happens as death has for Christians who die before it happens: it will be the end of life in this world and the start of life in what has been described as "an unknown environment with a well-known inhabitant" (cf. John 14:2-3). Christ teaches (Matt.

24:36-51) that it will be a tragic disaster if the *parousia* finds anyone in an unprepared state. Rather, the thought of what is to come should be constantly in our minds, encouraging us in our present Christian service (1 Cor. 15:58) and teaching us to live as it were on call, ready to go to meet Christ at any time (Matt. 25:1-13).

GENERAL RESURRECTION

THE DEAD IN CHRIST WILL RISE IN GLORY

But someone may ask, "How are the dead raised? With what kind of body will they come?" How foolish! What you sow does not come to life unless it dies. When you sow, you do not plant the body that will be, but just a seed. . . .
So will it be with the resurrection of the dead. The body that is sown is perishable, it is raised imperishable; it is sown in dishonor, it is raised in glory; it is sown in weakness, it is raised in power; it is sown a natural body, it is raised a spiritual body. . . .

1 CORINTHIANS 15:35-37, 42-44

✝ Jesus was the first to rise from the dead (Acts 26:23), and when he returns to this world he will raise his servants to a resurrection life like his own (1 Cor. 15:20-23; Phil. 3:20-21). He will, indeed, raise the whole human race; those who are not his through faith will be raised for sentencing (John 5:29). Christians alive at his coming will at that instant undergo a marvelous transformation (1 Cor. 15:50-54), while Christians who had died will experience a glorious re-embodiment (2 Cor. 5:1-5).

There will be continuity between the mortal and the immortal body, as there was in Jesus' case, for it was the body in which he had died that was raised. Paul compares the relation between the resurrection body and the mortal body to the relation between a seed and the plant that grows out of it (1 Cor. 15:35-44), a kind of continuity, we should note, that allows for great differences between the starting point and the end product. Also, says Paul, there will be in every case a contrast of quality. Our present bodies, like Adam's, are natural and earthly, subject to all sorts of weakness and decay until finally they perish. But our resurrection bodies, like Christ's, will be spiritual (created, indwelt, and sustained by the Holy Spirit) and will belong to the eternal, imperishable, immortal, heavenly order of things (1 Cor. 15:45-54).

However, as the risen Jesus was recognizable by his disciples despite the change that resurrection had wrought in him, and as the re-embodied Moses and Elijah were recognizable at the Transfiguration (Matt. 17:3-4), and as re-embodied Jewish saints were recognizable at the time of Jesus' rising (Matt. 27:52-53), so risen Christians will be recognizable to each other, and joyful reunions beyond this world with believers whom we loved and then lost through death are to be expected. That is implicit in 1 Thessalonians 4:13-18, which was written because persons who were alive in Christ feared they had finally lost those who had died in Christ; Paul wrote as he did about Christ's return in order to assure them that they would certainly see their Christian loved ones again.

As Jesus' single-minded love and humility are the model to which God is conforming our regenerate characters, so his glorified body, the present form of the body through which he perfectly expressed these qualities when he was on earth, is the model for the remaking of our bodies (Phil.

3:21). The bodies that Christians have now are at best poor tools for expressing the desires and purposes of regenerate hearts, and many of the weaknesses with which the saints struggle—shyness, shortness of temper, lust, depression, coolness in relationships, and so on—are closely linked with our physical constitution and its patterning in our behavior. The bodies that become ours in the general resurrection will be bodies that perfectly match our perfected regenerate characters and will prove perfect instruments for our holy self-expression throughout eternity.

Glorification (so called because it is a manifesting of God in our lives, 2 Cor. 3:18) is the scriptural name for God's completion of what he began when he regenerated us, namely, our moral and spiritual reconstruction so as to be perfectly and permanently conformed to Christ. Glorification is a work of transforming power whereby God finally turns us into sinless creatures in deathless bodies. The idea of our glorified final state includes (a) perfect knowledge of grace, through limitless extension of our powers of understanding (1 Cor. 13:12); (b) perfect enjoyment of seeing and being with the Father and the Son; (c) perfect worship and service of God out of a perfectly integrated nature and a heart set perfectly free for love and obedience; (d) perfect deliverance from all that is experienced as sinful, evil, weakening, and frustrating; (e) perfect fulfillment of all desires of which we are conscious (not sexual desire, Matt. 22:30; or hunger and thirst, Rev. 7:16; or desire for sleep, Rev. 22:5; but desires for more communion with God); (f) perfect completion of all that was good and valuable in this world's life but that had to be left incomplete because desire outran capacity; and (g) endless personal growth in the encompassing of all these perfect things.

Paul ends his analysis in Romans 8:30 of the action whereby God saves his elect with a striking past tense: "Those he justified, he also glorified." Glorification was in Paul's day, and still is, future for everyone apart from Jesus himself, but Paul's thought evidently is that since our glorification is here and now a fixed point in God's sovereign plan, it is already as good as done. The past tense is meant to let us know that it is absolutely impossible for our glorification not to happen. Such is the sureness and certainty of the Christian hope.

JUDGMENT SEAT

GOD WILL JUDGE ALL MANKIND

Then he will say to those on his left,
"Depart from me, you who are cursed,
into the eternal fire prepared for the devil
and his angels."

MATTHEW 25:41

✠ The certainty of final judgment forms the frame within which the New Testament message of saving grace is set. Paul in particular stresses this certainty, highlighting it to the sophisticated Athenians (Acts 17:30-31) and spelling it out in detail in the first section of Romans, the New Testament book that contains his fullest exposition of the gospel (Rom. 2:5-16). It is from "the coming wrath" on "the day of God's wrath, when his righteous judgment will be revealed," says Paul, that Jesus Christ saves us (1 Thess. 1:10; Rom. 2:5; cf. Rom. 5:9; Eph. 5:6; Col. 3:6; John 3:36; Rev. 6:17; 19:15). Throughout Scripture, God's *indignation, anger,* and *fury,* which are often spoken of, are judicial; these words always point to the holy Creator actively judging sin, just as *wrath* does here. The message of coming judgment for all mankind, with Jesus Christ completing the work of his mediatorial kingdom by acting as judge on his Father's behalf, runs throughout the New Testament (Matt. 13:40-43; 25:41-46; John 5:22-30; Acts 10:42; 2 Cor. 5:10; 2 Tim. 4:1; Heb.

9:27; 10:25-31; 12:23; 2 Pet. 3:7; Jude 6-7; Rev. 20:11-15). When Christ comes again and history is completed, all humans of all ages will be raised for judgment and will take their place before Christ's judgment seat. The event is unimaginable, no doubt, but human imagination is no measure of what a sovereign God can and will do.

At the judgment all will give account of themselves to God, and God through Christ "will give to each person according to what he has done" (Rom. 2:6; cf. Ps. 62:12; Matt. 16:27; 2 Cor. 5:10; Rev. 22:12). The regenerate, who as servants of Christ have learned to love righteousness and desire the glory of a holy heaven, will be acknowledged, and on the basis of Christ's atonement and merit on their behalf they will be awarded that which they seek. The rest will receive a destiny commensurate with the godless way of life they have chosen, and that destiny will come to them on the basis of their own demerit (Rom. 2:6-11). How much they knew of the will of God will be the standard by which their demerit is assessed (Matt. 11:20-24; Luke 11:42-48; Rom. 2:12).

The judgment will demonstrate, and so finally vindicate, the perfect justice of God. In a world of sinners, in which God has "let all nations go their own way" (Acts 14:16), it is no wonder that evil is rampant and that doubts arise as to whether God, if sovereign, can be just, or, if just, can be sovereign. But for God to judge justly is his glory, and the Last Judgment will be his final self-vindication against the suspicion that he has ceased to care about righteousness (Ps. 50:16-21; Rev. 6:10; 16:5-7; 19:1-5).

In the case of those who profess to be Christ's, review of their actual words and works (Matt. 12:36-37) will have the special point of uncovering the evidence that shows whether their profession is the fruit of an honest regener-ate heart (Matt. 12:33-35) or merely the parrot-cry of a hypocritical religiosity (Matt. 7:21-23). Everything about everybody will be exposed on Judgment Day (1 Cor. 4:5), and each will receive from God according to what he or she really is. Those whose professed faith did not express itself in a new life-style, marked by hatred of sin and works of loving service to God and others, will be lost (Matt. 18:23-35; 25:34-46; James 2:14-26).

Fallen angels (demons) will be judged on the last day (Matt. 8:29; Jude 6), and the saints will be involved in the process (1 Cor. 6:3), though Scripture does not reveal their precise role.

Knowledge of future judgment is always a summons to present repentance. Only the penitent will be prepared for judgment when it comes.

HELL

THE WICKED WILL BE BANISHED
INTO ENDLESS MISERY

*Then death and Hades were thrown into the
lake of fire. The lake of fire is the second
death. If anyone's name was not found
written in the book of life, he was thrown
into the lake of fire.*

REVELATION 20:14-15

✝ The sentimental secularism of modern Western
culture, with its exalted optimism about human nature, its shrunken idea of God, and its skepticism as to
whether personal morality really matters—in other words,
its decay of conscience—makes it hard for Christians to
take the reality of hell seriously. The revelation of hell in
Scripture assumes a depth of insight into divine holiness
and human and demonic sinfulness that most of us do not
have. However, the doctrine of hell appears in the New
Testament as a Christian essential, and we are called to try
to understand it as Jesus and his apostles did.

The New Testament views hell (*Gehenna*, as Jesus calls
it, the place of incineration, Matt. 5:22; 18:9) as the final
abode of those consigned to eternal punishment at the
Last Judgment (Matt. 25:41-46; Rev. 20:11-15). It is
thought of as a place of fire and darkness (Jude 7, 13), of
weeping and grinding of teeth (Matt. 8:12; 13:42, 50;

22:13; 24:51; 25:30), of destruction (2 Thess. 1:7-9; 2 Pet. 3:7; 1 Thess. 5:3), and of torment (Rev. 20:10; Luke 16:23)—in other words, of total distress and misery. If, as it seems, these terms are symbolic rather than literal (fire and darkness would be mutually exclusive in literal terms), we may be sure that the reality, which is beyond our imagining, exceeds the symbol in dreadfulness. New Testament teaching about hell is meant to appall us and strike us dumb with horror, assuring us that, as heaven will be better than we could dream, so hell will be worse than we can conceive. Such are the issues of eternity, which need now to be realistically faced.

The concept of hell is of a negative relationship to God, an experience not of his absence so much as of his presence in wrath and displeasure. The experience of God's anger as a consuming fire (Heb. 12:29), his righteous condemnation for defying him and clinging to the sins he loathes, and the deprivation of all that is valuable, pleasant, and worthwhile will be the shape of the experience of hell (Rom. 2:6, 8-9, 12). The concept is formed by systematically negating every element in the experience of God's goodness as believers know it through grace and as all mankind knows it through kindly providences (Acts 14:16-17; Ps. 104:10-30; Rom. 2:4). The reality, as was said above, will be more terrible than the concept; no one can imagine how bad hell will be.

Scripture envisages hell as unending (Jude 13; Rev. 20:10). Speculations about a "second chance" after death, or personal annihilation of the ungodly at some stage, have no biblical warrant.

Scripture sees hell as self-chosen; those in hell will realize that they sentenced themselves to it by loving darkness rather than light, choosing not to have their Creator as their Lord, preferring self-indulgent sin to self-denying righteousness, and (if they encountered the gospel) rejecting Jesus rather than coming to him (John 3:18-21; Rom. 1:18, 24, 26, 28, 32; 2:8; 2 Thess. 2:9-11). General revelation confronts all mankind with this issue, and from this standpoint hell appears as God's gesture of respect for human choice. All receive what they actually chose, either to be with God forever, worshiping him, or without God forever, worshiping themselves. Those who are in hell will know not only that for their doings they deserve it but also that in their hearts they chose it.

The purpose of Bible teaching about hell is to make us appreciate, thankfully embrace, and rationally prefer the grace of Christ that saves us from it (Matt. 5:29-30; 13:48-50). It is really a mercy to mankind that God in Scripture is so explicit about hell. We cannot now say that we have not been warned.

HEAVEN

GOD WILL WELCOME HIS PEOPLE
INTO EVERLASTING JOY

*Do not let your hearts be troubled. Trust in
God; trust also in me. In my Father's house
are many rooms; if it were not so, I would
have told you. I am going there to prepare a
place for you. And if I go and prepare a place
for you, I will come back and take you to be
with me that you also may be where I am.*

JOHN 14:1-3

✝ *Heaven*, which in both Hebrew and Greek is a word
meaning "sky," is the Bible term for God's home (Ps.
33:13-14; Matt. 6:9) where his throne is (Ps. 2:4); the place
of his presence to which the glorified Christ has returned
(Acts 1:11); where the church militant and triumphant
now unites for worship (Heb. 12:22-25); and where one
day Christ's people will be with their Savior forever (John
17:5, 24; 1 Thess. 4:16-17). It is pictured as a place of rest
(John 14:2), a city (Heb. 11:10), and a country (Heb.
11:16). At some future point, at the time of Christ's return
for judgment, it will take the form of a reconstructed
cosmos (2 Pet. 3:13; Rev. 21:1).

To think of heaven as a place is more right than
wrong, though the word could mislead. Heaven appears
in Scripture as a spatial reality that touches and inter-
penetrates all created space. In Ephesians, Paul locates

264

in heaven both the throne of Christ at the Father's right hand (Eph. 1:20) and the spiritual blessings and risen life in Christ of Christians (Eph. 1:3; 2:6). "The heavenly realms" in Eph. 1:3, 20; 2:6; 3:10; and 6:12 is a literary variant for "heaven." Paul alludes to an experience in the "third heaven" or "paradise" (2 Cor. 12:2, 4). No doubt the heaven of God's throne is to be distinguished from the heavenly realms occupied by hostile spiritual powers (Eph. 6:12). A resurrection body adapted to heaven's life awaits us (2 Cor. 5:1-8), and in that body we shall see the Father and the Son (Matt. 5:8; 1 John 3:2). But while we are in our present bodies, the realities of heaven are invisible and ordinarily imperceptible to us, and we know them only by faith (2 Cor. 4:18; 5:7). Yet the closeness to us of heaven and of its inhabitants, the Father, the Son, the Spirit, the holy angels, and the demonic spirits, must never be forgotten: for it is a matter of solid spiritual fact.

Scripture teaches us to form our notion of the life of heaven by (a) extrapolating from the less-than-perfect relationship that we now have with God the Father, the Son, and the Spirit, with other Christians, and with created things to the thought of a perfect relationship, free from all limitation, frustration, and failure; (b) eliminating from our idea of a life lived for God all forms of pain, evil, conflict, and distress, such as we experience here on earth; and (c) enriching our imaginings of that happy future by adding in every conception of excellence and God-given enjoyment that we know. The visions of heaven's life in Revelation 7:13-17 and 21:1–22:5 draw on all three of these ways of conceiving it.

According to Scripture, the constant joy of heaven's life for the redeemed will stem from (a) their vision of God in the face of Jesus Christ (Rev. 22:4); (b) their ongoing experience of Christ's love as he ministers to them (Rev. 7:17); (c) their fellowship with loved ones and the whole body of the redeemed; (d) the continued growth, maturing, learning, enrichment of abilities, and enlargement of powers that God has in store for them. The redeemed desire all these things, and without them their happiness could not be complete. But in heaven there will be no unfulfilled desires.

There will be different degrees of blessedness and reward in heaven. All will be blessed up to the limit of what they can receive, but capacities will vary just as they do in this world. As for rewards (an area in which present irresponsibility can bring permanent future loss: 1 Cor. 3:10-15), two points must be grasped. The first is that when God rewards our works he is crowning his own gifts, for it was only by grace that those works were done. The second is that essence of the reward in each case will be more of what the Christian desires most, namely, a deepening of his or her love-relationship with the Savior, which is the reality to which all the biblical imagery of honorific crowns and robes and feasts is pointing. The reward is parallel to the reward of courtship, which is the enriching of the love-relationship itself through marriage.

So the life of heavenly glory is a compound of seeing God in and through Christ and being loved by the Father and the Son, of rest (Rev. 14:13) and work (Rev. 7:15), of praise and worship (Rev. 7:9-10; 19:1-5), and of fellowship with the Lamb and the saints (Rev. 19:6-9).

Nor will it end (Rev. 22:5). Its eternity is part of its glory; endlessness, one might say, is the glory of glory.

Hearts on earth say in the course of a joyful experience,
"I don't want this ever to end." But it invariably does.
The hearts of those in heaven say,
"I want this to go on forever."
And it will. There can be
no better news
than this.